WILLIAM TEMPLE

AND

HIS MESSAGE

(A167)

PELICAN BOOKS

WILLIAM TEMPLE
and
HIS MESSAGE

Selections from his writings
arranged by
CANON A. E. BAKER
with memoir by the
BISHOP OF CHICHESTER

PENGUIN BOOKS

HARMONDSWORTH MIDDLESEX ENGLAND
245 FIFTH AVENUE NEW YORK U.S.A.

THE thanks of the editor and publishers are due to the Press
and Publications Board of the Church Assembly, for permission
to reprint two passages from *The Genius of the Church of
England ;* to the Epworth Press for two passages from *Social
Witness and Evangelism ;* to Hamish Hamilton Ltd. for several
extracts from *Basic Convictions ;* to the Lutterworth Press for
extracts from *One Lord, One People ;* to the Editor of the
Spectator for passages from an article, 'The Idea of God,'
which appeared in his pages on April 4th, 1931 ; to Macmillan
and Co., Ltd., and to Longmans Green and Co., Ltd., for
extracts from the books mentioned in the conclusion.

First Published in Penguin Books 1946

MADE AND PRINTED IN GREAT BRITAIN FOR PENGUIN BOOKS LIMITED
BY HUNT, BARNARD AND CO., LTD., LONDON AND AYLESBURY

NOTE

THIS book is issued in the belief that many who knew William Temple in some field or other of his far-ranging activities will be glad to have a brief Memoir, together with a selection of passages from his books and speeches. In writing the Memoir I gratefully acknowledge the help I have received, especially from Mrs. Temple. The selections have been made and arranged by Canon A. E. Baker of York. We both hope that all readers will look out for the official Biography of William Temple by F. A. Iremonger, Dean of Lichfield, which will be published in due course by the Oxford University Press, and will be led by the selections to William Temple's writings.

G. K. A. BELL
(*Bishop of Chichester*)

26th October, 1945.

CONTENTS

CONTENTS

MEMOIR

I

MEMOIR

WILLIAM TEMPLE was not only one of the greatest men of his day, but also one of the greatest teachers who have ever filled the Archbishopric of Canterbury. His tenure of the see was for no more than two and a half years ; yet his influence on the British people, in the field of social justice, on the Christian Church as a whole, and in international relations, was of a kind to which it would be very difficult to find a parallel in the history of England. It was no idle tribute that President Roosevelt paid, in expressing the sympathy of the American people, to the King—after the Archbishop's death, when he said ' As an ardent advocate of international co-operation based on Christian principles he exerted a profound influence throughout the world.' A whole series of qualities combined to give him this position. Some of them, it is hoped, will emerge from the study which follows : but it may be well to emphasise at the very start his astonishing vitality, his many-sidedness, his all-embracing humanity, and his serene and humble faith.

He was born at the Palace, Exeter, on October 15th, 1881, the second son of Frederick Temple, then Bishop of Exeter and already 59 years old, and Beatrice Lascelles, 24 years her husband's junior. William had a profound veneration for both his parents. Of his father, Archbishop of Canterbury 1897-1902, he said at his enthronement, ' He was and is among men the chief inspiration of my life.' He had an extraordinary intimacy with his mother, who survived her husband by just over 12 years.

His home life played an unusually important part in his

education ; and the *Memoir of Frederick Temple, by Seven Friends*, contains a whole series of letters from father to son, showing the intimate interchange of opinion, instruction and chaff, which went on over a number of years in his boyhood. He went to Colet Court, Hammersmith, as his preparatory school ; and thence to Rugby, with Dr. H. A. James as Headmaster. At Rugby he began his life-long friendship, which was to cover so wide a social and educational field, with R. H. Tawney, the well-known economist and historian, and J. L. Stocks (of Oxford, Manchester and Liverpool Universities).

In 1900 he went up to Balliol College, Oxford, with an Exhibition. There he took First Classes in the two Classical Honours Schools, was mentioned for the Ellerton Theological Essay, and became President of the Union. In 1904 he was elected to a Fellowship and Lecturership in philosophy at the Queen's College, Oxford. Here he read very widely, and amongst many other writers, English and foreign, made a special study of the works of S. Thomas Aquinas. He also spent part of 1906 studying at the University of Jena.

He had an astonishing memory, and could quote poetry without end, especially Browning and Shelley. It is at least from this time that we can date his power to remember, almost visually, the very page on which some particular passage occurred in a particular book that he had studied.

He delighted in the pastoral part of a tutor's work, and owed not a little to B. H. Streeter (later Provost of Queen's) on the religious side of College life. He was fond of walking with undergraduates, and took reading parties to the Lakes where, though never an athlete in the ordinary sense, he climbed the mountains with the utmost enthusiasm. He was famous from boyhood for his roars of laughter. He loved speaking at meetings of College and University societies of all kinds ; and he enjoyed music. He was always good company, and was well liked by his brother dons, though a senior Fellow, the Latin Scholar, A. C. Clark, noting Temple's frequent failure to remain for Common Room after High Table, shook his head somewhat ruefully now and then, with the remark that ' Temple has gone to the good.'

Two special interests developed while he was at Oxford. One was his deep concern in social problems. It began with work in a club, and indeed this beginning was characteristic of undergraduates of the day. ' The finest social work that I have seen,' he wrote in 1943, ' was the work of the Oxford and Bermondsey Mission,' with which he was closely associated between 1900 and 1910. Originally the club was opened in a disused warehouse in Abbey Street, Bermondsey, by a wonderful Doctor, J. H. Stansfeld, who was both parson and physician. It had a marked medical side, with which the training of boys and the teaching of religion was closely connected. Temple describes his first experience of the conduct of the Club in the following words :

' The Doctor's own methods were highly individual. The first time I visited the Club was during my second year at Oxford. I was taken into a basement room, where a crowd of some twenty people sat on benches round the wall ; one corner was screened off. The Doctor stood in the middle with myself just behind him, and preached with great directness for about five minutes. Then he turned abruptly and dived into the corner behind the screen, beckoning me to follow. We found a rickety table and three uninviting chairs. I sat on an end one and was given a pencil and a writing tablet ; the Doctor sat in the middle ; on the other chair sat the patients, one after another. With each a conversation took place on the following lines. " Put out your tongue. . . . Where did you go to church last Sunday ? . . . Open your mouth. . . . Why not ? Say ninety-nine. . . . Well, I'll give you some medicine, but mind you say your prayers and go to church in future."

The gaps represent inarticulate replies, the patient being in an attitude prohibitive of speech ; but the Doctor knew the answers without hearing. Then after I had sat there taking notes for him at his dictation after each had left, he suddenly said—" We must have finished the first lot by now and there will be another crowd ; go out and speak the Word to them for a few minutes." It was a Monday evening, so I recited what I could remember of a sermon preached in St. Paul's Cathedral by the Canon-in-Residence —Newbolt, I think—the day before. I cannot think what they made of it ; but the Doctor seemed satisfied.'

The second special interest which he maintained throughout his life was in educational reform. He was in strong revolt against anything which smacked of class distinction in the ancient Universities, and a champion, therefore, of the movement which sought to open the doors of his own University to students who could profit by the opportunities it offered, irrespective of class. He was one of the eight Oxford tutors who wrote to *The Times* on *Oxford and the Nation*, and so contributed to the Royal Commission on the Universities. It was at Oxford also that his close connection with the Workers' Educational Association began. Although not himself one of the actual founders, he was elected first President of the W.E.A. in 1908, at the instance of R. H. Tawney and Albert Mansbridge, and he remained President until 1924. From first to last he was unceasing in his devotion to its interests, never failing in his answers to the calls made on his time and ability, and whole-hearted in his enjoyment of its meetings and the innumerable friendships of which it was the source. It was here too that he entered upon his long and fruitful connection with the Student Christian Movement, mainly through the influence of Tissington Tatlow, who was its moving spirit, as well as its Secretary for many years. He constantly took large contingents of undergraduates from Queen's to the Student Movement Camps at Baslow during

the summer ; and in 1910, on the invitation of Dr. J. R.
Mott, he went on a tour to Australia, to speed the Student
Movement forward in that Commonwealth.

He was ordained deacon by Archbishop Davidson at
Canterbury in 1908, on the title of his fellowship, and priest
in 1909. The Archbishop became a ' second father ' to him,
and wisely decided that his theological views, which had
caused Francis Paget, Bishop of Oxford, some time earlier
to refuse him ordination, were not in fact so unorthodox
as to debar him.

One other field in which Temple was to play a great part
in the years that lay ahead was that of the World-wide
Church, and what became known later as the ' Oecumenical '
movement. He gave the first evidence of his concern
for this side of human and Christian action as an usher
at the International Missionary Conference at Edinburgh
in 1910. Three years later he became a member of the
first ' Archbishops' Committee ' on Faith and Order, and
was a regular attendant at its meetings from 1913 to 1920.

From Oxford he went in 1910 to be Headmaster of
Repton. One of his Repton colleagues writes :
' He was not really fitted, either by temperament or by
taste, to be a great headmaster, as he probably soon
discovered. He was never really interested in the adminis-
trative details of an educational institution, and he had
too many wider interests in the outside world to settle down
to them ; but, both in chapel and in the class-room, and
most of all perhaps in his familiar intercourse with the
senior boys, he was a source of real inspiration to many at
Repton. He made a host of life-long friends there, and his
Repton years were among the happiest in a fundamentally
happy life.'

He had already published his first book, *The Faith and
Modern Thought* (1910), before leaving Oxford. But it was
while he was Headmaster of Repton that he contributed an
essay on the Divinity of Christ to a volume entitled *Founda-*

tions (1912). This volume, with its sub-title, *A Statement of Christian Belief in Terms of Modern Thought : by Seven Oxford Men,* made a great stir at the time ; and it formed the subject of *Absolute and Abitofhell,* the famous Satire in the Manner of Mr. John Dryden by Father R. A. Knox, containing a portrait of Temple as the first and best known of the Essayists :

> ' First, from the Public Schools—Lernaean Bog—
> No paltry Bulwark, stood the Form of Og,
> A man so broad, to some he seem'd to be
> Not one, but all Mankind in Effigy :
> Who, brisk in Term, a Whirlwind in the Long,
> Did everything by turns, and nothing wrong,
> Bill'd at each Lecture-hall from Thames to Tyne
> As Thinker, Usher, Statesman, or Divine.
> Born in the Purple, swift he chose the Light,
> And Lambeth mark'd him for a Nazirite :
> Discerning Balliol snatch'd him in his teens,
> And mourn'd him, early forfeited to Queen's.
> His name suffic'd to leave th' insidious tome
> A household Word in every English Home :
> No academick Treatise, high and dry,
> Canvass'd in Walks round Mesopotamy,
> Or where in Common Room, when days are short,
> Soulless Professors gulp disgusted Port.
> " Not from the few, the learned, and the pale "
> —So rang his Message—" we expect our Sale ;
> Man in the Street, our Publication con—
> What matter, if the Street be Ashkelon ? " '

He left Repton to be Rector of S. James', Piccadilly, in 1914. While there he became for a short time a member of the Westminster Branch of the Labour Party, joining it in 1918. He took an active part, both before and during the war, in the production of *The Challenge,* a Christian weekly journal which had all too short a life. He also edited and contributed to a series of *Papers for Wartime,*

published by the Oxford University Press, and took part
in the discussions and manifestos issuing from a group of
friends of different denominations known as *The Collegium*,
in St. George's Square, under the inspiration of Lucy
Gardner, a Quaker.

In 1915 he paid his first visit to the U.S.A. to deliver the
Bishop Paddock Lectures on *Church and Nation*, in the
course of which he clearly laid down his view on the
relationship of Christianity to war, a view from which he
never diverged to the end of his life.

In 1916 he married Frances Anson. She and William
met as old family friends : but they had a common interest
besides in social reform, as she was for a time Secretary
of the Westminster Branch of the Christian Social Union,
of which he was Chairman, and also gave help in the office
of *The Challenge*. After a seven weeks' engagement the
wedding took place, and there can have been few happier
married lives than theirs.

The tenure of S. James', Piccadilly, did not last very
long. But the actual manner of leaving was critical for the
whole of Temple's later work for the Church. The National
Mission of Repentance and Hope (a large-scale evangelistic
campaign in all the dioceses of England and Wales) was
launched by the Archbishops of Canterbury and York in
1916. Temple was one of the Secretaries. In July of that
year the Archbishops' Commission on Church and State,
of which Lord Selborne was Chairman and Temple probably
the youngest member, published a unanimous report
advocating a considerable measure of legislative autonomy
for the Church of England. Dick Sheppard, Temple's
neighbour at S. Martin's-in-the-Fields, approached him one
day with this intriguing question, ' Don't you think we
ought to have a ginger group in the Church of England ? '
No sooner said than done. Temple, Sheppard, F. A.
Iremonger (Head of the Oxford House, Bethnal Green),
A. A. David (Headmaster of Rugby), Cyril Garbett (Vicar

of Portsea), and others to the number of 40 got together and started a movement with the inspired title of *Life and Liberty*, ' to win for the Church the liberty essential to fulness of life.' The movement was launched at a crowded and enthusiastic meeting in the Queen's Hall, in July, 1917, at which Temple presided. It carried a resolution urging the Archbishops to approach the Government ' without delay ' on the subject of freedom for the Church. There was one dissentient, Dr. Henson, whose tribute to Temple's oratory on the occasion is well worth quoting :

' Temple's speech was well-phrased and well-delivered. He has an admirable voice, and, though his manner is a little too dogmatic and professional, he is in the succession of orators.'

Three months later the Life and Liberty Council asked Temple to resign S. James's, Piccadilly, in order that he might be free to campaign throughout the country on behalf of liberty for the Church of England. Temple agreed, though it meant leaving his staff (of whom he was specially fond) at S. James's, giving up all certainty in his future career, and dropping from £2,000 to £700 a year in stipend. It was typical of him that he cared little about the last. For eighteen months, from January, 1918, to June, 1919, he travelled at a breathless pace all over England, founding and developing Life and Liberty fellowships, making speeches on Church and State, advocating not disestablishment, but a reformed establishment. It was an exhausting as well as an exhilarating experience. Combined with Viscount Wolmer's efforts in the House of Commons and in his Church Self-Government League outside, Temple's energy and convictions made a vital contribution to the success of the cause ; and everything was crowned by the sagacious and determined statesmanship of Archbishop Davidson. Thus was secured the final enactment of the Church Assembly (Powers) Measure, commonly known as the Enabling Bill, in 1919. This was a Measure

which in fact gave powers to a new Church Assembly
(composed of bishops, clergy and laity), enabling it to
undertake Church legislation by means of Measures which
were to have the effect of Acts of Parliament, subject only to
the simple Aye or No of both Houses of Parliament. The
way was thus at last opened for the achievement of many
long overdue reforms.

In June, 1919, Temple was appointed Canon of Westminster. Curiously enough, twice before he had been offered a
Westminster Canonry, once at Repton, when he was
disqualified as he had not been six years in Orders, and
once later. He became very fond of the Abbey, but soon
left his stall to succeed Dr. Knox as Bishop of Manchester,
in 1921. In this northern see he quickly made himself at
home, proving his deep concern for social progress and
education, loved by the clergy, and charming not a few,
whom his predecessor had found very difficult, by his
humour and ability. He delivered admirable Charges and
Presidential Addresses to his Diocesan Conferences on
theological and social themes. He was always ready to
speak at meetings of the W.E.A. He took an active part
in the annual Blackpool Missions, and was the life and soul
of the meetings and services on the sands and elsewhere.
It is also no small sign of the confidence he inspired that
in the field of diocesan organization his episcopate was
marked by the division of the diocese into the two dioceses
of Manchester and Blackburn. Thus in all sorts of ways,
in the city of Manchester, in the Lancashire towns, and in
Manchester University he made a deep impact on the
industrial life of the North.

There were outside calls also, of which three may be
mentioned. From 1920 to 1927 he edited The Pilgrim, a
Quarterly Review of Christian Politics and Religion. Many
of his own Essays in the Review are reprinted (together
with four Presidential Addresses to the Manchester
Diocesan Conference, before the diocese was divided) in

Essays in Christian Politics. As it was the purpose of *The Pilgrim* to present the Christian view on the various questions of the day, so the various essays and addresses, on subjects ranging from ' Christianity and Politics ' to ' Coué and S. Paul,' and ' the Resources of Literature,' showed the conclusions which their author had reached after testing his judgment by the touchstone of Christian principles. And it was characteristic of the range and consistency of his claims for the Christian religion that in the essay on ' Christianity and Politics ' he made it plain that ' no firm line can be drawn marking off those sides of public life and its ordering which properly concern the Church from those which do not.' ' Just because of its concern with individual character, the Church is vitally concerned with the conditions that affect character.' ' It has long been admitted,' he wrote, ' that the Church has a duty in relation to Housing and to Schools, for no one can doubt the effect which these have on character ! But it is impossible to stop here, or with Temperance or Gambling.

' No department of human life lies outside the scope of moral principle, and in none are the order of life and the maxims governing public action without influence on character. There is a frontier of the Church's legitimate concern, but it is not one that excludes any human interest ; it only defines the Church's method of dealing with that interest. The limitation of the Church's sphere is not a matter of area but of method.'

He urged then, as he urged to the end of his life, that even if Christianity were concerned with the individual only, it would still have to interest itself in politics for the sake of its work with individuals. But he further urged, with the same persistence, that Christianity must also ' criticise actual institutions in the light of its own social principles, because it aims, not at the salvation of individuals one by one, but at that perfect individual and social welfare, which is called the Kingdom of God or the Holy City.'

The fullest public expression at that time of this Christian-Political point of view was the inter-denominational Conference, of which he was the prime mover, known as the *Christian Conference on Politics, Economics and Citizenship* (COPEC) held at Birmingham in 1924. It was the first conference of its kind in which the Churches of Great Britain (apart from Rome) united in a common witness on economic, social, and political questions ; and had far-reaching results.

But Temple also intervened on concrete issues. An important illustration of such intervention in an industrial dispute is to be found in the coal strike of 1926. After it had gone on for several months a group of Bishops, of whom Temple was one, decided to try to bring the parties together. A Royal Commission had issued a Report, of which the recommendations had not been adopted. A deadlock had been reached, and bitterness was increasing. Nobody appeared to be taking any steps to bring the owners and the men together. So the Bishops came forward, not to propose any terms of their own, but to urge the frank adoption of the Report as a basis of settlement. This effort at mediation caused much comment. The Prime Minister, Mr. Baldwin, asked how the Bishops would like it if he referred to the Iron and Steel Federation the revision of the Athanasian Creed ; and this was acclaimed as a legitimate score! Both parties however accepted the invitation. The coal owners made no positive proposals. The miners put forward a suggestion which represented a method of bringing the Report into operation. The suggestion was rejected by the Government, who announced its rejection before receiving the deputation of Bishops and hearing what they had to say. When the effort failed, Temple, in a letter to *The Times* of August 20th, 1926, gave its history, and the principles on which it was based. He concluded his letter as follows :

' If it is urged that such action as we took is improper

in principle, we completely disagree with such a view. As Christians, and most of us as Christians charged with official responsibility, we saw two parties doing great injury to the community by a continued conflict, which was bound to be ended by negotiation sooner or later ; our religion and our office required of us that we should do anything which lay in our power to bring them, in the literal sense, to reason. We never imagined either that we could suggest satisfactory terms of our own or that economic facts can be modified by humane sentiments. But we felt a responsibility for trying to secure that the settlement should be not only economically sound in itself, but reached with the minimum of bitterness or resentment and the maximum of good will. Whether the particular steps which we took to discharge this responsibility were wise or foolish is another question, not for us to answer. I will not mention that, while the policy of the " slogan " was bound to be withdrawn sooner or later, it was in fact at the conference with one group that the withdrawal took place. And if we be still accused of acting for the miners and not for the owners, we reply that this is only because the miners did, and the owners did not, reach proposals in conference with us based on the Report and showing a readiness to substitute reason for force as the arbiter of the dispute.'

While Bishop of Manchester he conducted a University Mission at Cambridge, in 1926. He conducted other University Missions later, in particular one at Oxford in 1931, and another at Dublin in 1934. Their theme was ' Christian Faith and Life.' Those who were present at any of these Missions, and now look back on their experience in listening, testify not only to the intellectual but to the profound spiritual impression made. As one of them, Eric Abbott (now Dean of King's College, London), who was an undergraduate at Cambridge, and Undermissioner at Dublin, puts it:

' The words—which were never short of the highest intellectual level and made a fully intellectual demand upon the sustained attention of his hearers—had in them a rare quality of spiritual passion and of deep devotion.'

The fact that stood out before everything else was Prayer, Temple's own prayer, his concern for the prayer of others, and his rating of prayer more highly than any other activity whatsoever. The intellectual substance of the Mission can be recovered from the book of published addresses, *Christian Faith and Life ;* but what is harder to recover is the quite extraordinary impression Temple made of a man entirely integrated in mind and soul through the Christian faith.

The Rev. F. R. Barry (now Bishop of Southwell) was Vicar of S. Mary the Virgin, Oxford, when the Oxford Mission took place, and what he writes about it is assuredly true of Cambridge and Dublin as well :

' I think it was one of the high lights in his ministry because it established him in an undisputed primacy of leadership and confidence among young people. It was a turning point in the life of post-war Oxford. It " stopped the rot" and re-established the Christian faith in the centre of the thought and life of the University, and its influence continues. There are many men and women doing conspicuous Christian service, both in Great Britain and overseas, who owe their vocation and inspiration to that week. In many ways it really was one of his greatest achievements—though of course he would insist that it wasn't him at all.'

In November, 1928, Archbishop Lang succeeded Archbishop Davidson as Archbishop of Canterbury. Temple was appointed as Dr. Lang's successor in the Archbishopric of York. Here he was extraordinarily happy. The demands of York were heavier than those of Manchester, but they still left time for other avocations, and gave Temple a new vantage point. He was now able to speak with an official

authority in the Church of England second only to that of
the Archbishop of Canterbury. He became an intimate
friend of his brother Primate, and retained the rooms in
Lollards' Tower, Lambeth Palace, which Davidson had
given him in 1924, as Bishop of Manchester, throughout the
whole of his time at York.

He loved his diocese, and worked it in a remarkably
co-operative spirit with his staff. He preached and spoke
everywhere, but always keeping a special place in his
affections for Bishopthorpe itself, church and village alike.
Few Bishops called out a greater loyalty from their clergy
and colleagues. He cared nothing for extremes in Church
opinion. Neither extreme, he said, could save the soul of
England. At York, as also at Manchester, he showed the
deepest personal interest in his ordination candidates, and
the relation between the young deacon or priest and
William Temple as ordaining Bishop was for ever afterwards one of the most precious things in the former's life.
Everything was controlled by a spirit of prayer ; nor
could anyone who saw him in the Chapel at Bishopthorpe
at Embertide fail to see that to him prayer was the essential
factor in the life of a Christian, and therefore especially in
the life of a priest.

He made friends with all classes, and when he moved
to Canterbury the people of York felt it as a personal loss.
He was a little shy, perhaps, of the squire, and county
folk ; but with young people and large audiences he got on
famously. At Christmas time he thoroughly enjoyed the
household parties at Bishopthorpe, dancing Sir Roger with
any who came, and beaming on whoever sat next to him at
table (the places being chosen by lot on these occasions).
There were also in 1939 two parties for railwaymen and their
wives from York Station, who were entertained at Bishopthorpe, seventy at a time. Bishopthorpe itself was used
extensively for conferences of all kinds, international,
economic, and theological ; and also for gatherings of the

Girls' Diocesan Association—these including the particularly enviable feature of charades, in which Temple took
a full and uproarious share.

He had been at Bishopthorpe for hardly more than a
year and a half when the seventh decennial Lambeth Conference of the Bishops of the Anglican communion was held
in 1930. It was the first Lambeth Conference he had
attended. He was Chairman of the Committee on Christian
Unity. Most of the proceedings of the Committee were
devoted, by force of circumstances, partly to a proposed
plan of Church union in South India ; partly to a series of
negotiations with representatives of the Eastern Orthodox
Churches. Under his guidance the proposals for unity in
South India were helped forward by a favouring wind,
though not without an indication of those elements in the
proposals which were likely to give rise to controversy.
It was probably a real disappointment to Temple that,
mainly because of the pressure of the South India proposals
on the non-Episcopal side, very little time was given to the
consideration of the relations between the Church of
England and the non-Episcopal Churches in Britain,
which had so important a place in the Lambeth Conference
of 1920. But at all stages of the Conference Temple's
ability and wise leadership made a powerful contribution.
On the personal side, no member was more popular or more
hospitable. Almost every week he entertained parties of
overseas Bishops and their wives at Bishopthorpe.

Following the first Anglo-Catholic Congress in 1920, and
perhaps hastened by the controversial discussions at a
conference of Modern churchmen at Oxford on the general
subject of Christ and the Creed, Archbishops Davidson
and Lang appointed a Commission in 1923 ' to consider
the nature and grounds of Christian Doctrine with a view
to demonstrating the extent of existing agreement within
the Church of England, and with a view to investigating
how far it is possible to remove or diminish existing differ-

ences.' Dr. Burge, Bishop of Oxford, was its first Chairman, but on his death in 1925 Temple took his place. For the next twelve years he took an active part in the framing of the Report. He enjoyed the stimulus of the argument between advocates of very different schools of thought. He took particular delight in the meetings of the Northern group of members at Bishopthorpe, and the incisive and admirably good-humoured debates between Oliver Quick, L. S. Thornton, A. E. J. Rawlinson, C. J. Shebbeare and others. When the Report appeared, under the title *Doctrine in the Church of England* (1938), it owed more to his constructive thought, conciliatory temper, and skilful pen (for he was a master at drafting, as he was also a master at chairmanship), than to anyone else ; and while it was not a finished treatise, or a full statement of the Anglican position generally, it gave a wise, lucid and comprehensive exposition of Anglican thought in some very important fields of theology.

In 1934 he published his Gifford Lectures, *Nature, Man and God.* He had already produced two striking volumes of Christian philosophy, *Mens Creatrix* in 1917, and *Christus Veritas* in 1924. The Gifford Lectures were of a more substantial order, and though he had covenanted with the Gifford Trustees, when he received their invitation, that he could only give what was already in his mind, without special reading, on publication they were generally welcomed as work of a very high order, admirable if they had come from a University Professor, astonishing when the magnitude of the author's activities in public life was remembered.

It was in these same years that Temple's leadership in the general Oecumenical movement in the Church grew more and more powerful. As we have already seen, his share in it began when he was at Oxford. He himself traced the origin of the Oecumenical movement to the great missionary enterprise of the last 150 years. Although his interest in the application of Christian principles by the Churches in partnership to the social system was of long standing, his initiation into the Oecumenical movement actually came from the side of Faith and Order, that is the theological study of the relations of the different Churches, through their differences as well as their agreement, as proposed by the American Episcopal Church in 1910.

His principal connection with the Faith and Order movement from the international angle dates from his attendance at the first World Conference on Faith and Order at Lausanne in 1925. Here he took a considerable part, and was much called on in the drafting of reports. Bishop C. H. Brent, of Western New York, was Chairman at Lausanne, and became Chairman also of the Continuation Committee, of which Temple was a member. On the death of Bishop Brent in 1929 Temple was elected Chairman, at the meeting at Maloja, and from that time on he continously held the foremost place. He regularly attended the meetings of the Committee, in whatever part of Europe they were held. He presided over the second World Conference on Faith and Order held at Edinburgh in 1937 ; with a courtesy and a clarity which contributed in an extraordinary degree to its success. In the earlier part of the same summer another world conference on Church, Community and State took place at Oxford, representing the other (' Life and Work ') aspect of the Oecumenical movement. Here he was a member of the section dealing with the *Una Sancta* and the World of Nations. His main contribution however was in drafting the message of the Conference. For this he had to read the draft reports of five sections, discuss particular points with selected members, and make a single whole. It cost him much labour, far into the night : but the result was generally acclaimed.

There was however a particular matter, in which both these Conferences were concerned, where his leadership was invaluable for the future of the Oecumenical movement. It was the bringing together of the two streams of the same movement into a single river. What was known as the Committee of 35, consisting of representatives of both sides, agreed to recommend that the two sections, Life and Work (Oxford), and Faith and Order (Edinburgh), should be merged in a single World Council of Churches. Their recommendation was accepted by both Conferences. An agreed constitution for the new World Council was approved by a conference of delegates at Utrecht in 1938. Temple became Chairman of the Provisional Committee of the World Council, the complete formation of which has been delayed by the war. He was its inspiration from first to last, attending all the meetings, and giving steady support and counsel to the executive officers. Its basis is a common belief in Jesus Christ as God and Saviour. It is indeed the greatest potential organ for world-wide fellowship of Christians outside the Church of Rome now in existence. And already 88 churches of different communions have accepted membership. ' Almost incidentally,' he said at his enthronement at Canterbury in 1942, ' the great world-fellowship has arisen ; it is the great new fact of our era ; it makes itself apparent from time to time in World Conferences such as in the last twenty years have been held in Stockholm (1925), Lausanne (1927), Jerusalem (1928), Oxford (1937), Edinburgh (1937), Madras (1937), Amsterdam (1939).'

Among all these conferences, except Stockholm and Madras, William Temple had been present as a personal leader. But his oecumenical spirit was shown in other ways too. In December, 1935, he went to the United States for the second time. The centre of his visit, which lasted five weeks, was a Student Volunteer Conference at Indianapolis (January, 1936), where he gave three addresses, and led a seminar on War and Peace. He also gave different series of lectures at the College of Preachers in Washington

rejected pacifism, as he always had, without a moment's hesitation. But he still retained his friendship with pacifists, and went out of his way to attend meetings of the Cloister Group, composed of both pacifists and non-pacifists, and delighted in the hospitality of Canon Charles Raven, Master of Christ's College, Cambridge, in whose Lodge the group often gathered. At the same time, his oecumenical experiences, as well as his large human sympathy, led him to welcome proposals which, without compromise of principle, might shorten the war. Thus he went, with three other British churchmen, to Holland in January 1940, in order to meet French, Dutch, Scandinavian, Swiss, and American Church leaders ; and to try both to express the oecumenical conscience and to find some way of translating it into action. Bishop Berggrav was one of the prime movers in the same enterprise, and at the end of the discussions took with him to Berlin a memorandum approved by the Archbishop of York, Henry Carter, William Paton and the Bishop of Chichester. The memorandum, accompanied by a message to a similar effect from Pastor Marc Boegner, President of the French Protestant Church Federation, was hardly even looked at by the German authorities; and Bishop Berggrav went back to Oslo through England with the knowledge that nothing could be done. Hitler was clearly seen to be determined on war to the bitter end.

All through the war years Temple insisted on the ideal basis of the Allied cause, and denounced Fascism as a sinister idolatry. As Chairman of a Peace Aims Group of laymen and ministers in Britain, of which William Paton was the clear-headed and energetic Secretary, Temple kept in close touch with the American Commission to Study the Bases of a Just and Durable Peace, over which John Foster Dulles presided; and when the Commission produced its statement of political propositions, commonly known as *The Six Pillars of Peace*, he and thirteen other British

Church leaders published their comments in a statement
entitled *A Christian Basis for Reconstruction.*

He looked forward to the time after the Allied victory; and
in his hopes for the future he required both a short-term and
a long term policy regarding the Germans. There should, he
said, be ' such expression of moral condemnation of recent
German policy as cannot fail to bring home to the people
of that land what is the moral judgment of the world concerning them. On the other hand there must be, in the long-
term policy, provision that the coming generation shall be
able to recognise the position given them in the world as
a fair one.' And besides the task of education, and besides
looking forward to renewed fellowship, he said, ' we must
take care that the long-term settlement secures for the
ordinary German citizen of future generations an even
chance of sharing in the benefits of civilisation, provided
his State is behaving as a good neighbour.'

Still, during the war, writings of different kinds continued
to pour forth. The two Series of *Readings in S. John's
Gospel* appeared in 1939 and 1940—the fruits of a life-time
of meditation, which had begun in a series of sermons given
in S. James', Piccadilly, in which Temple as rector had gone
right through the Fourth Gospel, chapter by chapter, every
Sunday for nearly four years.

One of the most notable events in which Temple took
part during the first half of the war was the Malvern Conference of January 1941. The Conference, attended by
some 200 Bishops, clergy and lay members of the Church
of England, was called in order to ' consider from the
Anglican point of view what are the fundamental facts
which are directly relevant to the ordering of the new
society, and how Christian thought can be shaped to play
a leading part in the reconstruction'. It aroused an even
greater interest in America than it did in Great Britain. But
what impressed the British public was that here, in the middle
of the war, a great body of Anglican churchmen should

put out a social message representing the mind both of the
younger and the older leaders which, by its simplicity, its
vigour, and its brevity made it plain that the social issue
was a burning issue for the Church of England, and could
never again be put in the background, while men like
Temple proclaimed it. Its findings, published as *The Life
of the Church and the Order of Society*, were largely the
drafting of the Archbishop as Chairman. Its first Proposition was an endorsement of the Ten Points put forward in
a joint letter to *The Times* of December 23rd, 1940, which
the Archbishops of Canterbury and York, Cardinal
Hinsley, and the Rev. W. H. Armstrong (Moderator of the
Evangelical Free Church Council) signed, with the general
title ' Foundations of Peace'. All the Propositions were
presented to the Conference, and taken as agreed if no
objection was raised. But there was one substantial Proposition which, after various amendments, was put in a form
agreed by its own movers (headed by Sir Richard Acland,
M.P.) and the movers of the amendments to it, and carried
by a full vote of the whole Conference without any hostile
vote, though some abstained from voting. In view of its
general importance, and its relevance to Temple's teaching,
it is here printed in full :—

' God Himself is the Sovereign of all human life ; all
men are His children, and ought to be brothers of one
another ; through Christ the Redeemer they can become
what they ought to be.

' There can be no advance towards a more Christian way
of life except through a wider and fuller acceptance of
this faith, and through the adoption, by individuals, of the
way of living which it implies.

' There is no structural organisation of society which can
bring about the coming of the Kingdom of God on earth,
since it is a gift of God, and since all systems can be perverted by the selfishness of man. Therefore, the Church
as such can never commit itself to any proposed change in

B—WT

the structure of society as being a self-sufficient means of salvation.

'But the Church can point to those features of our existing society which, while they can never prevent individual men and women from becoming Christian, are contrary to divine justice, and act as stumbling-blocks, making it harder for men to live Christian lives.

'In our present situation we believe that the maintenance of that part of the structure of our society, by which the ultimate ownership of the principal industrial resources of the community can be vested in the hands of private owners, may be such a stumbling-block. On the one hand it may deprive the poorest members of the community of the essentials of life. On the other, while these resources can be so owned, men will strive for their ownership for themselves. As a consequence, a way of life founded on the supremacy of the economic motive will remain, which is contrary to God's plan for mankind.

'For one or both of these reasons, the time has come for Christians to proclaim the need for striving towards a form of society in which, while the essential value of the individual human personality is preserved, the continuance of these abuses will be no longer possible.

'Members of the Church of England, clergy and laity alike, cannot take part in this work unless they are ready to advocate and being about a complete change in the internal financial position of the Church of England.'

Later in the same year Temple published *Christianity and Social Order* as a Penguin Special. Small though it is, it stands out as one of the most persuasive and lucid statements of the Church's attitude to the social system, as Temple viewed it. It had a very wide circulation, not only in the British Isles, but in the U.S.A., the Dominions, Scandinavia, and other countries to which English books had access. It dealt with the right of the Church to interfere, the method the Church should use, the history of Church intervention ; and it laid down primary Christian social principles, viz., (1) God and His Purpose, (2) Man : his Dignity, Tragedy and Destiny ; and derivative Christian social principles, viz., (1) Freedom, (2) Social Fellowship, and (3) Service. Incidentally Temple refers in the Penguin to an Archbishop of Canterbury in the seventeenth century, Archbishop Laud, as a great social reformer. ' Archbishop Laud,' he said, ' owed much of his unpopularity with the section of society then represented in Parliament to his vigorous action, often high-handed, in checking the robbery of the poor by the encroachment of landlords and the " enclosing " of common lands. He stood for the older social ethics of a peasant civilisation.'

In 1942 Dr. Lang decided that the time had come for him to resign his office, and allow his successor opportunity to prepare for the post-war years, and the Lambeth Conference which was due to be held soon after the establishment of peace. The fall of Singapore caused some delay in the announcement of his successor. There was known to be strong opposition in certain quarters, but Mr. Churchill yielded to the urgent recommendation of Dr. Lang, supported in almost every part of the Church, and by the general verdict of the nation, and nominated William Temple as ninety-ninth Archbishop of Canterbury. His enthronement took place in Canterbury Cathedral on S. George's Day, 1942. Immediately afterwards Temple threw himself into the work of his great office with courage and energy. Lambeth Palace had already been badly blitzed, and while keeping a few rooms at Lambeth both for office purposes and as a small home, he and his wife made the Old Palace, Canterbury, their headquarters, from which they continually went up for the greater part of the week to London. He was at Canterbury when the first of the three great bombing raids took place on June 1st, 1942, and won the affection of Canterbury citizens by returning, during the week that followed, on every night when his urgent business in London made it possible. At Lambeth itself, in the summer of 1944, he was in the thick of the flying bombs, one of which missed Lambeth Palace by less than 150 yards.

The autumn of 1942 saw the launching of a campaign with the general title 'The Church looks forward ', proclaiming Christ as the Lord of all life. Beginning in the Albert Hall on September 26th, 1942, he and his successor at York (Dr. Garbett) together held a series of meetings in London, Birmingham, Leicester and Edinburgh for the express purpose of affirming ' the right and duty of the Church to declare its judgment upon social facts and social movements and to lay down principles which should govern the ordering of society '. From a variety of angles he bade men see the supremacy in all respects of the Human Person. ' It has always been recognised, of course ', he said, ' that the Christian religion has its message for the life of the individual within the framework of society. We are concerned to insist that it also has its message for the ordering of society itself, and that the social structure, as well as the lives of individuals living within that structure, is subject to criticism in the light of Christian principles.' He encountered a good deal of criticism for his bold claim that Christ ruled politics; and at times he may have taken an injudicious step in the details of his remarks on credit or banking. But it should be remembered that while he often talked publicly about credit, and sought to secure the public control both of the volume of credit, and the direction in which it is issued, what he wanted was that people should be forced to think about the subject, and not regard it as taboo.. ' I have talked about credit before ; but people do not always like it talked about. I do not ask you to believe anything I say about it ; but I do ask you to think about it.'

Like every bold speaker, he was often misrepresented. This was particularly the case in what he was supposed to teach about the profit motive. He objected to its pre-dominance, he did not condemn it in itself. ' There is no harm in the profit motive as such,' he said, ' It has its own right place, but that is not the first place. And it is the predominance of the profit motive—the fact that it comes first in the determination of so much of our economic and industrial activity that is a great evil ' (*The Church Looks Forward*, p. 109).

The campaign, which ended with a Youth Rally in London on October 3rd, 1943, was (like the Malvern Conference) under the auspices of the Church of England, working through the Industrial Christian Fellowship. But Temple was just as eager to give his witness on an inter-denominational platform. Many of the interdenominational meetings at which he spoke were known as ' Religion and Life ' meetings. It was a new form of evangelism. And wherever he went, he had a wonderful reception. When the ' British Council of Churches ' was formed in September 1943, he presided at its first meeting, and was elected its first President. And, in preaching the inaugural sermon in S. Paul's Cathedral, he thus explained the character of the co-operation for which the Council of Churches stood :—

' There is no compromise of our distinctive principles in our coming together. But there is a choice involved between two different directions of attention, two different points of emphasis. In days when Christianity itself in its funda-mental principles is unchallenged it may seem natural to lay most emphasis on the points which distinguish one communion from another. But in days like these when the basic principles of Christianity are widely challenged and in many quarters expressly repudiated, the primary need is for clear and united testimony to Christianity itself. The difference between Catholic and Protestant is very small as compared with the difference between Christian and non-Christian, between those who do and those who do not believe that in Jesus Christ God hath visited and redeemed His people.'

Side by side with this work of leadership in the social crusade, Temple played an active part in the discussions in and out of Parliament on the Education Act, 1943. It was in no small measure due to his influence, and the trust reposed in him not only by the President of the Board of Education, Mr. R. A. Butler, but by educationalists generally, and by Free Church leaders, that there was no recurrence of the old bitter religious controversies.

As Archbishop of Canterbury he also befriended the cause of the Jewish and Non-Aryan Christian refugees from Nazi oppression. Together with the Archbishop of Westminster, the Moderators of the Church of Scotland and the Free Church Federal Council, and the Chief Rabbi, he assisted in the formation of a Council of Christians and Jews. And in another field, also humanitarian, he did his best (though he failed) to persuade the Government, in the House of Lords in 1944, to permit the passing of powdered milk and vitamins through the blockade for the relief of children and invalids in Belgium and Greece. In March, 1944, he took occasion to express his views on the treatment of Germany, following the long and sustained bombing of German cities. In a preface to a pamphlet by Stephen Hobhouse, *Christ and our Enemies*, he wrote :

' To me it seemed at an earlier stage of the war that the peace terms must for a limited period include a penal element, if justice were to be done. But the intensification of the bombing of German cities seems to me to have altered that. Those of us who believe that this intense bombing is justified as a military measure, aiming at the checking of Germany's power to produce war material, must also recognise that it constitutes a penalty for German aggression so great that no other can be called for. . . . Anyhow, whatever may be appropriate as a policy for the prevention of future aggression and the establishment of security in Europe, or as an execution of justice in relation to some individuals, any thoughts of " punishing Germany ", more than the course of the war is punishing her, must henceforth be excluded from the minds of those who are under obligation to find and to follow the way of Christ.'

Month by month there were the incessant claims of provincial administration, and the care of all the churches, which falls on the shoulders of the Archbishop of Canterbury, besides the demands for University and other Sermons, for speeches and broadcasts, and for visits to the troops and the Fleet. He took great pains with his Presidential Addresses to the full Synod of the Southern Convocation, and was an encouraging as well as business-like chairman at Bishops' Meetings. There was also his own diocese of Canterbury, with all its problems, and the preaching Sunday by Sunday in town and country parishes in East Kent and Croydon. He loved the diocese. He loved the Cathedral. Both he had known as a boy. And he greatly enjoyed his regular meetings with his staff, in which he again displayed a singular gift for calling forth the loyal co-operation of every member.

From early childhood Temple had always been subject to gout : and right through his life he was liable to sudden disabling and sometimes lengthy attacks. In the late summer of 1944 an attack of more than usual severity laid him low. Its full force showed itself at Canterbury in September, and he was obliged to remain almost entirely in bed. He was however able to take the chair at a week-end conference, consisting mainly of laymen, at the Old Palace, on *The Purpose of God in Society*. His last public engagement (as it proved to be) was to address, for an hour, the clergy of the diocese assembled in Canterbury Cathedral (into which he had to be carried in a chair), on the vital subject of Evangelism. Soon afterwards he was taken to a hotel in Westgate. Here he still kept in touch with some of his work, and only four days before the end was able to see Bishop Oldham of Albany, and Bishop Hobson of Southern Ohio, who had come from the United States. None of those about him knew how serious his condition was ; and he himself, on the Monday before he died, sent a message to his diocese to say that he believed he had now turned the corner. But on Thursday, October 26th, the end came with unexpected suddenness. He said to his wife, ' I feel very faint '. A heart-specialist who happened to be in the hotel was hastily summoned, and did all that was possible, but a thrombosis had set in, and after twenty minutes' or half an hour's breathlessness he died.

So closed the earthly course of a great Archbishop of Canterbury. He had once said that he dreaded the thought of slowly dying, and was happily spared that, as he was spared a long spell of invalid existence. On All Saints Eve, October 31st, he was laid to rest in the cloister garth of Canterbury Cathedral.

There have been great figures among his predecessors at Canterbury. He was just 63 years old. But in the short two and a half years Temple had won, as all men felt, a place among the greatest. To the ordinary man it seemed a tragedy that the unique work he appeared destined to accomplish for the Church, for the nation, and for Christianity throughout the world, should be thus cut short. Thousands, in all walks of life, felt his going as a personal loss. People of every kind, in the Church and out of it, in the Forces, in the W.E.A., and in all sorts of groups and organisations, mourned him just because he was what he was, and because they knew he was prepared to fight for things that they believed in.

It is difficult to convey any adequate notion of his general appearance. He was 5 ft. 9½ ins. tall. As a boy he was fat, and when he was grown up the impression that a superficial observer might easily get was of a robust stoutness. There is at least one picture of him, of which Bishop Gore said, ' This is nothing but the portrait of a fat man!' But though he had bulk, nobody who knew him well, indeed nobody who had watched him at his work, mistook that as a dominant feature. It was his look that struck one most of all—a clear, somewhat round face, with blue-grey eyes both piercing and kind. He always wore glasses in a light gold frame, quite inconspicuous. The impression he gave was of great stillness and gentleness, combined with extraordinary power. His hair was rather fair, with no trace of grey yet showing. When he had gout he walked with a stick, bravely and firmly : but when in his ordinary health he stood and walked erect. He was tidy in his dress, correct on official occasions, never fussy, and on holidays very ready to relax in an old tweed suit. Like his father he was a non-smoker and a total abstainer. It is true that he was extremely fond of sweet things, but being well aware of the danger which sweet things are to a gouty subject, he knew how to check himself. All his life he laughed loud and long. But as he grew older, though his laugh never left him, there was a growing gravity in his look, and in wartime an increasing sense of the sorrows of the world.

His holidays were a special delight to him, and part of the secret of his abundant energy is found in the plans he made to secure real holidays, while he worked incessantly outside them. Not that his holidays were times of indolence; for it was in them that he wrote some of his books, and several hours of every day had to be given to letters. From the time he became a Bishop, he nearly always had a fortnight at Christmas, a fortnight at Easter, a month or six weeks in the summer, and occasionally a week in October. Much of this time he spent in the Lake District, for which he had a passion ; and he walked incessantly, with Buttermere, and latterly Grasmere, as favourite headquarters. As a young man, he liked nothing better than running down a steep path with a crowd of companions, jumping from stone to stone, and roaring with laughter. For the last twelve years of his life he made a haunt of the

Quantocks ; and in earlier days he had other favourite places, particularly Ramsbury in Wiltshire, and Totland Bay in the Isle of Wight. In the last two years he grew fond of Singleton, near Chichester. Dingestow Court, Monmouth, the home of his wife's brother-in-law and sister, Sir Ronald and Lady Bosanquet, was a favourite haunt ; and for many years William preached in the village church on the last Sunday of the old year or the first Sunday of the new. Latterly he loved reading aloud to his wife when on holiday, and was particularly fond of Dickens and Browning. He took a mass of books away with him, light and heavy, especially books on European history ; but however stiff his reading, he never had to take notes, so amazing was his memory.

His married life was most happy, and mention has already been made of his profound love for his parents. He was also devoted to his friends, some of whom have already been named. The closest were those of his school and university days. He was particularly drawn to the young, and loved talking to them, both individually and in groups. He was in his element in the Oxford Union, for example, as a one-man Brains Trust on a Sunday afternoon as Archbishop of Canterbury, organised by the University Political Societies, delighting in the swift rush of questions and answers. He was not always so obviously at ease with older men. Surprising as it may seem, to some of his contemporaries, and to official people, he often appeared formidable. But there were a few among his seniors for whom he had a special affection. One was Charles Gore, of whom he saw a good deal at Woolbeding in Sussex, where he stayed with his aunt, Mrs. Lascelles, Gore's sister. Others were Cosmo Gordon Lang, and Randall Davidson, his immediate predecessors at Canterbury : and ' Jimmy ' Palmer (Bishop of Bombay) who had been Chaplain at Balliol and meant much to him from Balliol days onwards.

He was very humble about himself, and far readier to

see the good than the weak points in others. He may have thought too well of men. He had a disarming innocence about him, and it was hard for him to form a harsh judgment, just as it was hard for him to say No to those who asked his help or favour for their projects. He had at times his opponents, but he never had an enemy. He had certainly a great gift of sympathy. ' No-one could go to him in times of trouble or sorrow,' said Lord Cranborne in a tribute which he paid in the House of Lords, ' and not be comforted by his robust faith ; and where comfort was wanted, there he was always to be found. I remember very well meeting him at one of the great railway stations in London in the early days of the war. There had been a heavy raid on Hull and he was on his way to give consolation to the afflicted people. I shall never forget the sight of that sturdy figure in episcopal apron and gaiters, with a tin helmet slung over his arm. There, I felt, was the Church militant. And indeed he had many qualities of a crusader. He was brave, he was resolute, he was above all young in spirit.'

As this brief memoir draws to a close, it is not easy to put into a few words the outstanding characteristics of a man so versatile, so human, and possessed of such genius. But it can be truthfully said that he was pre-eminently a prophet, that is ' one who speaks for God as the inspired revealer or interpreter of His will.' He was a teacher projecting the fruits of his Christian faith into various spheres, He had an uncommon talent for exposition, and for presenting the great themes of Christian philosophy and theology to almost any kind of audience. He was most powerful in great mixed meetings of all classes, such as he was continually called on to address. He was singularly effective in broadcasts and in conveying his personality to millions on the air. He was unsurpassed with undergraduate audiences and congregations. He was no less excellent with a Diocesan Conference. He had a fine voice : but his whole manner was quiet, and without gesture. Some of

his most striking achievements seemed almost effortless !
Those who heard him lecture on S. Thomas Aquinas, to a
learned Roman Catholic Society in October 1943, will
remember the extraordinary admiration with which the
experts heard this busy Archbishop of Canterbury expound
the Thomist philosophy, relying only on the notes he had
pencilled on the back of an envelope. Nor did he fail in
humility. President Van Dusen, of the Union Theological
Seminary in New York, tells how once, in 1935, after
Temple had delivered a course of lectures on Christology,
and said he had ten minutes in which to answer questions,
one of the audience asked him why he dealt almost entirely
with the divinity of our Lord, seeming to ignore the
humanity. He replied that he had done so because that was
what the New Testament did. Then he corrected himself,
saying, ' No, I am wrong. The New Testament emphasises
the two sides equally. I see that I must reconsider my
lecture.'

As we have noted, it was Temple's constant aim to
insist that the Christian faith demanded expression in the
social and political realm. The Church had in the past
concerned itself very actively with these questions. It had
developed a very complete system of principles by which
those who were responsible for the public ordering of life
might be guided. For some three hundred years, for a
variety of reasons, this whole area of human activity had
been evacuated by the Church. The recovery of the lost
ground was vital. Temple utterly repudiated the view that
religion was only concerned with heaven. That view has
sometimes very crude expressions. Most crude were those
of the Nazis, who offered ' freedom ' to the Churches in
Germany and in the occupied countries on the one condition that ' you will only talk of soul and heaven : you
will leave body and earth to us.' But the same view is also
current, in politer forms, in Great Britain. Instances have
already been quoted, from Mr. Stanley Baldwin and Mr.

Neville Chamberlain ; and there are many in high political positions, and in all walks of life, who think of or quote our Lord's words ' My kingdom is not of this world ' in a way entirely inconsistent with our Lord's mission on earth, and with an entire forgetfulness of the clause in our Lord's Prayer, ' Thy kingdom come on earth as it is in heaven.' To Temple all life was one, and there was no single acre in the whole human territory where the commandments of Christ did not hold good. When Temple claimed that Christian principles must apply to economics and politics, he was simply asserting that, as economics and politics were a very important part of man's daily life, they should be governed by Christian principles. The religious and the political interests of a man could not possibly be kept in watertight compartments. The truth was that Temple was more aware than most churchmen of the tremendous influence which the social structure has on men's character. He therefore saw the political factor as often the vital factor, and decisions in the political field as crucial. But he was not a party politician. In this field too he was a teacher, stimulating men's consciences, not dictating how men should vote.

At the same time, as a stimulator of men's consciences, Temple exerted a profound influence on the whole attitude of the nation to social problems. A remarkable tribute is paid to this influence by the well-known Italian Roman Catholic writer, Ernesto Buonaiuti, in *La Nuova Europa*, August 19th, 1945, in an article on ' English Religious Life and the War.' After a reference to the repercussions of the war on the religious and spiritual life of the various belligerents, he speaks of the new attitude taken by the Churches of Great Britain. They approved of the freedom of scientific research. Pronouncements on social problems became more courageous ; and it was this latter fact, Buonaiuti says, which had contributed most effectively to the Labour victory, and prepared the way to the social reforms the Government was planning. The Anglican Church had her own man of providence in this, William Temple. Though Temple died before the end of the war and the ' silent revolution,' according to Buonaiuti he was an effective co-operator in both. ' As president of the Workers' Educational Association he came into close contact with the working classes. Through this kind of daily contact, Archbishop Temple conceived such a clear vision of the new social problems and their inseparable inclusion in the problems of British national freedom, to be in a position, if necessary, to pronounce himself efficiently on the complex development of the spiritual life on the continent.'

What are we to say of his relation to the ordinary business of the Church ? Here too he was the prophet, rather than the administrator. He was greatly interested in the relations of Church and State ; but concerned himself with large principles far more than with details of organisation. Thus he was not an active initiator of specific Church reforms. And if the Life and Liberty campaign is quoted as evidence to the contrary, that after all was mainly, in his hands, a prophetic movement. And as to the question of Establishment, he took the view that this was not the direct concern of the Church as such, but was the concern of the State. ' If you are going in for Disestablishment,' he said at Birmingham, with reference to a question asked by Sir Stafford Cripps, ' it is an immensely intricate process ; and a good many of us are going to be tied up, for five or ten years to come, merely to adjusting the machinery of the Church, and not getting on with our real job.' That real job, in his judgment, is evangelism : an evangelism of which, in the present century, social witness is an indispensable instrument.

If Temple's function in the ordinary business of the Church of England was that of the prophet and the teacher, he filled this same role in an outstanding manner with regard to the Universal Church. He was above all the prophet of the Universal Church. He gave his witness to this as the leader of the Oecumenical movement of the last 35 years, among the Churches outside the Roman obedience, a movement which is doing so much to emphasise the agreements which unite Christians, and to overcome their divisions. He did not suppose unity (a very different thing from uniformity) would come quickly between the non-Roman Churches ; and he had the utmost respect for diversity and integrity of tradition. In the World Council of Churches (in process of formation) he saw a good omen for the future, just because the Council, while respecting the differences in various communions, based co-operation between the Churches on the common faith of Christians in Jesus Christ as God and Saviour.

The historian will determine the magnitude of the role which William Temple filled in contemporary life. Yet this at least may be said. He was not only a British but a world figure. He may have made mistakes in particular judgments or policies, or in the details of administration. But he had what are more important and rarer qualities in a Church leader—vision, imagination and courage. He was a man of extraordinary intellectual and spiritual power, as well as of extraordinary industry. He never spared himself, though he never gave the impression of haste. And in the midst of his activity he kept the serenity and simplicity of a child. ' Ministers of good things,' said Richard Hooker, ' are like torches, a light to others, waste and destruction to themselves.' William Temple had all the vividness and swiftness of a flame. It was like a flame that he sped through our whole firmament, filling every corner of it with a new splendour. It was like a flame that he communicated warmth and light to all who saw or heard him. We cannot expect to look upon his like again in our lifetime.

PREFACE

NEVER before has an Archbishop of Canterbury published so much. Dr. Temple's message for the Church and the world is to be found in all sorts of publications—in the Gifford Lectures and other works of technical philosophy and theology, in many smaller books intended for a more popular constituency, in a very large number of pamphlets, addresses, and magazine articles, and in introductions to other people's books. The total bulk is somewhat formidable—there are more than seventy items under his name in the British Museum catalogue—and there is, of course, a considerable amount of repetition. But this collection of extracts from his writings has been prepared in order to make his teaching readily available for all who want it.

It is not an anthology of great and beautiful passages ; there are many of these in his works, and there is certainly room for such an anthology. And considerations of space have necessitated the omission of much that deserved a place here. There is nothing of his exceedingly interesting literary criticism—the things that delighted him most, from Homer to Browning and Dostoyevsky, as well as his frank justification of his dislikes—or of his tastes in music. I should have liked to be able to quote some of his appreciations of great and good men, such as Archbishop Davidson, and to reproduce in full some of his sermons. His teaching on war and peace has had to be omitted ; the general principles of it are well known, and he did not foresee anything like the actual present situation.

In spite of the omissions, the extracts present the remarkable variety and comprehensiveness of a mind unique in the breadth of its knowledge and the sure penetration of its insight. Most people who read this book will find that the William Temple they have known and read is some aspects of the whole man. He was a philosopher, a theologian, a social teacher, an educational reformer, the oecumenical leader, and the Primate of All England. And in all these things he was a devout Christian, a simple believer in goodness, speaking of God to the hearts of common men.

A. E. BAKER.

N.B. *References at the foot of each extract are to code letters identifying books, in accordance with the index at the end.*

SELECTIONS FROM
HIS WRITINGS

SELECTIONS FROM HIS WRITINGS

HOW LIKE WILLIAM TEMPLE

FIRST there is a number of passages which recall the man as he talked and lived among us ; they are characteristic of him :

' The cynic who goes into the world determined to trust men no further than he can see them and to use them as pawns in his own game, will find that experience confirms his prejudice ; for to such a man men will not show the finer sides of their nature. The Christian, who goes into the world full of love and trust, will equally find that experience confirms his " prejudice," for to him men will show the finer and more sensitive sides of their nature, and even where there was no generosity his love and trust will, at least sometimes, create it. But though each finds his view verified the latter has the truer view, for he sees all that the other sees and more besides.' H. vol. I, p. 134.

' It may be true that we have exaggerated the importance of sport ; but there is a healthy instinct behind that, because a game is an end in itself, at any rate if you really play it as a game. There are some people who turn games into a business, when the poison has got really deep into their system. But the object of a game is the game : there is nothing beyond it. When you begin looking for something beyond it, then you are ruining it. The reason why I gave up golf was that I began to wonder why I should care whether the ball went into the hole or not. It generally didn't. Well once you begin to question, the game is ruined. You have got to take it mystically, or not at all ;

for it is an end in itself. Politics are never an end in themselves. The whole arena of politics belong to a class of activities which is less important than the class to which games belong.' Ae. 119.

' When people invite you to take a safe course they always mean the same thing—that you should select some disaster which is not the worst possible, and involve yourself in it. Thus you have safety against the worst which might otherwise befall you. But you can only play for safety by repudiating the ideal. The pursuit of the ideal is always fraught with peril.' Ai. pp. 79, 80.

' It is not natural to man to prefer the general good to his own ; Indeed, that is a description of what in one word is called Salvation.' Y. p. 183.

' The principles of ethics have as their end the perfect character and the perfect society ; and in this spontaneity finds a place, so that the end of ethics itself condemns a rigid and mechanical application of its principles. It is even a good thing to realise the mastery of these principles by occasional deliberate breach of them if only to escape from slavery to them.' Ab. p. 127.

' Mr. Proud says, " I don't care what you think of me " ; Mr. Vain says, " I wonder what you are thinking of me." Both are occupied with their relation to other people's opinion of them. The humble (which means " Objectively-minded ") man does what has to be done with all his attention fixed upon it. He is neither consciously indifferent to other people's opinion nor consciously anxious about it. If his task is to act upon other people he will be very much concerned with their opinions, for to mould (or to help them in moulding) their opinions is the task in hand ; if his task is to " kill the ball " at lawn tennis or to sing a great song, or to win a war, his mind will be utterly given to the task and spectators or critics will be as though they were not. But the last illustration introduces a new element, in so far as to win a war it is necessary to retain the con-

fidence of the people ; so criticism will receive attention,
not because the man is interested in other folks' opinion
of himself but because he has to carry them with him if he
is to accomplish his task.   For all achievement some
measure of humility or self-forgetfulness is indispensable ;
for the highest achievement the humility must be perfect.'
Ab. p. 139.

' . . . in History, I may know all the dates of all the
events that ever happened and still have no real historical
knowledge. For what matters is not when anything happened, but why it happened when it did.' L. p. 238.

' The man who has really faced the terrors of life in
Macbeth, or its horrors in *Othello*, or its dim mystery in
Hamlet, or its vast grey gloom shot through with fires of
anguish in *King Lear*, and has seen all this redeemed by
beauty so that its very fearfulness becomes an element in
its sublimity, should be a braver man from that day forth.'
Ab. p. 164.

' It is definitely undesirable to develop the intellectual
powers of a man who has not learnt how to be a member
of society. If a man is going to be a villain in heaven's
name let him remain a fool. But if the social purpose is to
be formed in him, then he needs intellectual training to
make that purpose effective. As a matter of fact, we suffer
far more from stupidity than from deliberate wickedness,
and tend to forget that alertness of mind is a necessary
part of moral goodness. It is not, of course, requisite that
everybody should be clever, but it is requisite that everybody should be sensible and mentally honest.' L. p. 237.

' Self-contentment is the death of vital religion. And we
easily become self-contented, at least as regards large areas
of our life, because our faith has saved us from most of the
acts which the common standard of society condemns, but
has not so far penetrated us as to force us to judge ourselves
always and only by the standard of Christ. So though we
know with our minds that self-complacency and perdition

are inseparable, if not indistinguishable, we nevertheless become self-complacent.' F. February, 1934.

' All else is to be valued because, and only because, it leads men to the feet of Jesus Christ, and aids their loyalty to His allegiance. Our first concern is with nothing on earth at all, whether Church, or Creed, or Sacrament, or Order, it is to uphold before men's hearts and minds and consciences and wills the claim of Jesus Christ as Lord upon their obedience, their trust, their love.' Au.

' His miracles are fulfilments of expectation created by ancient prophecies, and therefore contain in themselves His claim to be the promised Messiah. But they are all works of love ; they are all manifestations of power sub-ordinated to love. Is that not almost a definition of the Kingdom of God—power subordinate to love ? " All power corrupts." The one thing that can save power from being a source of corruption is its subordination to love, so that it is used always and only as love directs.' Ax. p. 27.

' No Christian will ever dream of saying " It is his own fault, now let him suffer for it." If Christ had taken that line, where would our redemption be ? He will say, rather, " If it is not his own fault, there is not much to trouble about. We have only to put him on his legs again, and it will be all done. But if it is his own fault—poor fellow, what can we do to help him ? " ' Aa. p. 82.

' By belief in a proposition I mean the determination to act as a man would if he knew it were true.' Ay.

' My ignorance of all things scientific is so immense as to be distinguished.' S. p. 1.

' Numbers are to me of all things the most elusive (my own method of finding the sum of a series of numbers, for instance in doing my accounts, may be poetically described in this way : I add them up and then I add them down, and then I split the difference between the two results so reached).' S. p. 8.

' There is no charm in the whole realm of art so subtle, so

intangible, so ethereal as that of music. It is the most spiritual and incalculable of all modes of expression.' S. p. 8.

'One of the motives which leads men to make their religion consist of rules is the hope that one day they will have kept all the rules, and then they may be free to please themselves. The law said that men should give one-tenth of their goods to God, and then they were free to use the rest as they liked ; but what the spirit requires is that we should never spend a penny except as God desires it to be spent. St. Peter at one time hoped to obtain some rule or regulation which he might satisfy, and then be free, concerning that duty on which our Lord laid such stress all through His teaching—the duty of forgiving enemies, forgiving those who injure us. He asks if seven times will do ; seven times is a great many, but he is told that it will not suffice, and four hundred and ninety times is suggested instead. That means there is to be no limit to forgiveness. The whole aim of St. Peter's question was not to be stimulated to forgive his brother seven times but to be freed from the duty of forgiving him at all, when he had done so the seven times demanded by the law. The religion of the spirit requires forgiveness for evermore because the spirit is love, and love will always want to forgive.' AF. p. 2.

'The Forgiveness of Sins is an article of the Creed ; that is to say it is one of the constituent parts into which the whole organic body of Christian faith may be articulated. All the articles of the creed name objects of practical trust. When a man says " I believe in God " he ought not to mean that after a careful review of the evidence he inclines to the opinion that there probably exists a Being who may not improperly be called God ; he ought to mean " I put my trust in God ; I am determined to live in reliance on His love and power." So the Christian trusts in Jesus Christ, and in the Holy Spirit, and in the universal Church, and in the fellowship of the saints, and in the resurrection

of the body and the life everlasting. He is determined to
live by confident reliance on all these. So, too, when he says
that he believes in the forgiveness of sins, he ought not
to mean that he holds the opinion that God forgives sins,
but that he believes in forgiving sins as a principle of
practical life—God's life and man's. He puts trust in God's
forgiving love ; but trusting that as good, he must needs
imitate it ; and therefore he trusts also the excellence and
power of forgiveness in human affairs. For as we have
seen, and as our Lord has taught us, God's forgiveness of us
cannot be separated from our forgiveness of one another.
We must forgive even as God forgives.' O. pp. 266, 267.

ST. THOMAS AQUINAS

In 1943 the Aquinas Society invited the Archbishop to
address it, and on October 19th he lectured to a crowded
audience in the Caxton Hall, Westminster, on *Thomism
and Modern Needs*. It was a historic event. The editor of
Blackfriars, the Dominican review, said that it placed
Catholic theologians and philosophers under a serious
obligation to consider the points raised in order to bring
Thomism into closer touch with modern problems, and
to fashion it into an instrument which will bring understanding between Catholics and others. Father Victor
White, O.P., one of the distinguished Thomists who heard
the lecture, later wrote of the many services which Dr.
Temple had rendered to Thomists by his address. It was
delivered from notes which were no more than headings.
Characteristically, the Archbishop destroyed these as
soon as the address had been delivered. But, characteristically again, when the Editor of *Blackfriars* asked that
he should write as an article for that Review the substance
of his address, he readily did so. These are some extracts
from it :

'I must make clear at the outset that I am not in any serious sense a student of St. Thomas—as, for example, my father was. I have read a considerable portion of his writings with close attention, but without that perpetual comparison of one passage with another which is alone entitled to be called " study " in relation to any great writer.' Ak. p. 86.

'It is not sufficiently understood in England that on the European continent this (admitting or repudiating the possibility of Natural Theology and the value of analogical argument from created nature, including human nature, to the nature of the Creator) more than anything else is the point at issue between Protestantism and Catholicism. The Continental Reformers had so interpreted the Fall of Man as to leave in fallen human nature no capacity for recognising divine truth ; all faculties were vitiated ; and between fallen human nature and the divine incorruption no analogy was possible. This finds its logical expression in the doctrine of Karl Barth that any man's response to divine revelation is as much a miracle as the occurrence of the revelation itself. God's impact on the world, for this view, is vertical only ; there is no horizontal guidance of man through the process of nature, including his own, or through the movement of history.' Ak. pp. 87, 88.

'The new emergence of individuality and consequently of responsible citizenship has led the modern world, so far as it is deeply religious, to a profounder understanding of sin. It is, I think, characteristic of the Reformation, as contrasted with the mediæval tradition and the Counter-Reformation, that it gave a new emphasis to Sin as distinct from sins. Perhaps perspectives have been damaged by the fact that so much of Moral Theology has been written under the impulse of a desire to meet the needs of Confessors and Spiritual Directors for guidance in their difficult and delicate task. The matter of confession is conscious sin recognised as such ; and this is bound to be for the most part particular rather than general. The penitent confesses sinfulness in general and passes at once to the particular sins which he is conscious that he has committed. So the Moral Theologian, in his proper desire to help, is liable to be content with a perfunctory definition of sin and proceed at once to its particular manifestations. Thus he concentrates attention on objective acts of sin from which the penitent by confession dissociates himself, and thereby directs attention from the essential sin which is the perversion of will issuing in those acts. This easily tends in practice to an unconscious Pelagianism—which I still regard as " the only heresy which is intrinsically damnable." For the suggestion is easily given that if we can find the right spiritual and psychological technique for remedying what we have seen to be wrong, we can put ourselves right with God.

' There is no trace of this in St. Thomas himself—quite the contrary—and so far as there is need for modification of his teaching here it is rather in its manner than in its content. But at this point the quasi-mathematical method of exposition is inevitably misleading. Its merit is a clarity achieved by the elimination of rhetoric or any emotional element. It is thus unable to express that tragedy of human nature to which Luther made men once more alive. Certainly we need to recover the sense or feeling—not only the intellectual conviction—of utter impotence to respond to the divine will, and of complete dependence for all power to serve God upon the divine grace. Whatever may be true of St. Thomas himself, the Thomist tradition as commonly presented does not adequately convey the awful pervasiveness and penetrating potency of sin in all departments of human life, including in its sphere of poisonous influence even our worship and our generosity.' Ak. pp. 90, 91.

REALISM

Dr. Temple was a realist, in the sense in which modern philosophers use that word.

' It is easy to say that we can only know what falls within our own experience, and of course this is so ; but when it is argued from this that the mind knows primarily its own ideas and from them infers a world outside, a grievous fallacy is introduced. An idea is not an object of the mind standing somewhere between the mind itself and the reality which it would know ; an idea is a mental apprehension of reality ; it may be adequate or inadequate, just as the image on the retina of the eye may be correct or incorrect according to the health of the whole eye ; if it is incorrect we see the object amiss, but it is perfect nonsense to say that what we see is the image on the retina ; this is the one thing which we never see at all, for it is that by which we see anything. . . . If we begin with the notion that the mind never has any objects except its own ideas, we can never argue to a world at all. Reality is the presupposition of all thinking ; in actual fact, the distinction between mind and its objects is drawn within the given *totum* of experience, and we have knowledge of the object or not-self before we have any knowledge of the subject or self. Self-knowledge, even knowledge of our own existence, is more inferential than knowledge of the world about us, just as, in its content, it is, as a rule, far more rudimentary.' L. pp. 50, 51.

Although he said that in his judgment too much attention is usually paid to the controversy between realism and idealism, as compared with other problems, he was, very definitely, not an idealist.

' Of course, I share the conviction at which Descartes arrived ; when I doubt, I cannot doubt that I doubt ;

even though I should doubt all else, I could not doubt myself as the subject of that doubt ; that, as a matter of psychology, is true. But to me it seems that in fact I cannot really doubt all else except myself ; I cannot really doubt the earth, or the stars, or (above all) my friends ; so that I cannot find in fact any greater psychological assurance about the existence of myself than about the existence of a great deal else. And there seems no reason to regard the assurance at which Descartes arrived as more than psychological. . . . It is impossible to think without thinking something. The subjective function of thought can be properly and usefully distinguished from every object of thought taken separately ; but it cannot be isolated from all objects of thought whatsoever without ceasing to exist.' M. p. 64.

' What Descartes indulged in his stove was purely academic doubt ; he was really as sure of the stove as of himself. If it be urged that this academic doubt was not an empirical absence of assurance but an " ideal supposal," I must reply that this method is permissible enough, but that Descartes found the wrong residuum. What he ought to have reached as the irreducible basis of all thought, including doubt, was the subject-object relationship. Then all the subsequent trouble would have been avoided. . . . What it represented when Descartes embarked upon it was the total collapse of the authority of mediæval tradition.' M. p. 66.

DIALECTIC

Dr. Temple was not only a realist, however, he was a dialectical realist. His first systematic study of philosophy was at Balliol when Edward Caird was Master, to whom, he said, he owed ' such grasp of the principles of Dialectic ' as he had acquired. And, of course, Dialectic was very much ' in the air ' when, in 1934, his Gifford Lectures were published.

' I believe that the Dialectical Materialism of Marx, Engels and Lenin has so strong an appeal to the minds of many of our contemporaries, and has so strong a foundation in contemporary experience, that only a Dialectic more comprehensive in its range of apprehension and more thorough in its appreciation of the interplay of factors in the real world, can overthrow it or seriously modify it as a guide to action.'   M. pp. 9, 10.

The notion of Dialectic, indeed, was fundamental to his thinking. In 1916 he wrote that the Dialectical movement is the vital process of thought.

' We may summarise it (the essential quality and method of the intellect) in this way ; contradiction is at once its enemy and its stimulus. It finds incoherence in its apprehension at any given time and reorganises its content to remove that incoherence. Contradiction is what it cannot think ; and yet contradiction is what makes it think. So by the perpetual discovery of new contradiction it is forced on to a more and more systematic apprehension.'

One of his favourite illustrations of the dialectic process was the specialisation of modern culture—in which the condition of knowing something about everything but not much about anything has been succeeded by knowing more and more about less and less. This ' modern ' way of thinking is, of course, the *antithesis* to the mediæval *thesis*—a premature and too complete unification of knowledge, so successful that any advance in knowledge or thought became possible only by breaking up the system already achieved. What is to happen now ? The development of the last four centuries cannot be merely scrapped. There can be no return to the pre-Renaissance position ; history does not work that way. The *synthesis*—and what in detail it will be cannot be foreseen, because it will be a new thing—will take up into itself, but transformed, what was valuable in the mediæval achievement, and what has been gained in the modern development. The account of this which the Archbishop wrote for the *University of Toronto Quarterly* demands very full quotation :

' The modern world has manifestly lost its way. Every department of life is infected with futility, except so far as it represents an interest isolated from the general concern of men. It is true that Science is pursuing its all-conquering course, subjecting one observed phenomenon after another to its regnant hypotheses, and imposing upon the innocent public an ever more paradoxical interpretation of what had seemed to be simple experiences. Yet when all this triumphant knowledge is pressed into the service of human needs, it produces more chaos than ever, and is more fruitful in making war appalling than in making peace enjoyable. Indeed, we have reached a stage of so-called human progress in which we are likely to go to war because we are so much afraid of doing so and to become involved in universal poverty because it is easy to produce abundant wealth. . . .

' The mediæval unification sought to allot to every departmental activity its appropriate sphere. The great merit of that effort was its determination to see each department in the light of the whole ; its fatal defect was the attempt to control the activity of the departments, not by the persuasive influence of the spirit of the whole, but by regulations which were, or seemed to be, external. Politics, Art, Science, Philosophy, were right to refuse all dictation from Theology. It was natural, though calamitous, that this refusal should take shape as a claim to absolute autonomy. So Politics reverted to the pagan principle, *Salus reipublicae suprema lex*, and the natural national State made claim to an allegiance due by right only to God. Art broke loose from one attachment after another until it degenerated into the artist's self-expression without regard to any question whether that self was worthy, or even fit, to be expressed. Science dissolved into the sciences, each pushing so far its independence of others that its subject matter is reduced to pure abstraction—a measurement of dimensions but not of things. Philosophy, no longer able to take for its field the inter-relation of all aspects of experience because each was repudiating its relation to the rest, attempted to construct an interpretation of reality from the starting point of bare self-consciousness ; and Theology, a Queen bereft of subjects, could only mourn her isolation as she brooded over a religion reduced to " what a man does with his solitariness." It is small wonder that in the upshot our " modern world " is like a rudderless ship on a stormy sea. There is an abundance of pilots, indeed, each with a different chart, a different goal, and an idiosyncratic compass. We all agree that the world is in a mess ; but there is no agreement about the road to recovery because there is no agreement as to the meaning or destiny of human life, the scale of values, or the power of man to rescue himself from his predicament. Never has there been so much knowledge of the means to the good life, both physical and psychological ; never has there been a greater sense of futility and frustration, because we cannot agree upon the conception of the good life itself.

' This state of things is not to be remedied by any mere return to mediævalism. We may look back with admiration to men whose scheme of life was so clear-cut and so complete ; but we could not endure the actualities of mediæval life. Moreover, we can see in the principle of the mediæval scheme the cause of its failure. It was an attempt to reach Heaven by a short cut, and establish the Kingdom of God on earth by making His Church a super-state. Thus the political impulse was driven into resistance to the spiritual, and the spiritual belied its own character in order to coerce the political. Above all, we must recognise that the emphasis laid by Luther and Descartes

C—WT

on personal integrity in apprehension of, and witness to, truth, was pure gain. We cannot go behind that. . . .

' The world is feeling its way back to unity. . . . Can we lay down any condition for the success of this movement ? . . . This article is written with the sole purpose of urging that we can, and that the condition is to be found precisely where the " modern " world is least likely to look for it. The chaos of our world arises from the indefinitely multifarious varieties of human temperament, the divergent tendencies of different national and racial cultures, the discrepancy in the estimate of Good and Evil formed by different men and different peoples. What hope can there be of bringing these together ? What is likely, for example, to emerge from the joint efforts of a Chinese Confucian, a Burmese Buddhist, an Indian Hindu, an Arabian Moslem, a German Nazi, and an American Behaviourist ? Is it not clear that they could agree only upon platitudes too insignificant to be worth disputing ? No one human tradition can attain to an expression of itself which can command the adherence of the followers of other traditions ; no amalgam of them all can have the definiteness that gives to any conviction its motive force. If there is to be found a principle of solution for our perplexities, it must be found elsewhere than in the consciousness of men ; it must be found in that most unpopular of quarters—a Divine Revelation. . . .

' If God exists, then, because He is Creator of the world and " Determiner of Destiny," the welfare of man consists in conformity with His will. If He has revealed Himself, that revelation will supply the standard for all judgments upon acts done or contemplated. If He is revealed as the Father of all men, and as being essentially Love, then in His revealed purpose is the principle which can bring together in harmony all persons of all races. There is no apparent hope of finding such a principle elsewhere.

' The yearning of the world for unity can be satisfied

only by a divine self-revelation. But if we believe that we have received such a revelation, we must avoid the mediæval blunder of attempting to coerce conformity with it. We must point to it as our criterion ; we must test our own conduct and aspiration and purpose by reference to it ; we must proclaim the way of hope for men and nations which seems to us to flow from acceptance of it. And then we must leave the world to accept or reject it by the action of reason and affection. For only the spiritual appeal which wins a voluntary assent penetrates deeply enough to control the secret springs of life. It is better to fail for the moment because our testimony is rejected than to win success by infecting with worldliness the call of the Spirit. But we may, indeed, we must challenge all who hope for some restoration of the unity of life with the question where they may reasonably hope to find the principle of that unity. And if it be true that only a divine revelation affords any such hope, then we must point to the revelation which we believe to have been given, and call men to think out again their several problems with added help of its illumination. But we must not only or chiefly call others to do these things ; nor can we wait till they answer. We must do the best we can, ourselves and at once. This is a shocking conclusion for an article in an academic magazine. But if shocks are what men need why not administer them ? ' Ah.

SCIENCE

It was by the aid of Dialectic that he justified the reality of value and, in particular, of faith in God, in a universe which, as science describes it, began billions of years before the first finite mind was produced within it. In so far as Dialectic is valid, values and faith must be included by the philosophers as carefully as the data of physics and

chemistry. Far too much modern thought has been content
to take the universe as science describes it as real, while
treating intuitions of truth, beauty and goodness—and
faith in God—as uninvited interlopers. Dr. Temple pointed
out the absurdity of this :

' The question is whether Faith is justified ; and philosophers have set themselves to answer this by considering
the universal cogency of established yet ever advancing
mathematics, the presuppositions of triumphant physics,
the new demands of self-confident though still speculative
biology—anything and everything in fact except Faith
itself. Before a man says his prayers he is to gain permission to do so from a philosophy which, in deciding
whether to grant such permission or not, considers everything except those same prayers. What wonder that Faith
and Philosophy have tended to drift apart ! ' M. p. 11.

He saw that the fundamental error is

' the conviction that the simple contains the explanation
of the complex, which leads to the denial of objective
reality to aesthetic and moral qualities because these only
appear at a stage of high development and advanced com-
plexity." M. p. 86.

And later in the book he summed up his criticism of this
position :

' If we begin with mindless and valueless fact we cannot
give any place in our scheme to Mind or Value without
breaking up the unity of the scheme itself. The very activity
which makes science possible remains unaccounted for in
the theory of the world which men have constructed in the
activity of science. It cannot be unscientific to prefer an
alternative approach by which we may at least hope to
find a place for science itself in its own world.' M. p. 216.

During nearly forty years he came again and again to
the criticism of the philosophy of science. In 1904 he printed
' for private circulation ' a paper on *The Province of Science*
he had read to the Oxford Junior Scientific Club. From

beginning to end its theme is that the only explanation the natural sciences can give of the world is bound to be inadequate.

' Science aims at explaining the world—that is, at making it satisfactory to the mind, or giving an account of it with which the mind can rest content. But the mind is not only logical, but also moral, and will not be content with an account of the world which does not demonstrate its morality.

' Science aims at explaining the world—that is, at reducing its differing particulars to a single principle : but it must not confine itself to the mechanical world and set up the Idol of Uniformity. Mind too is one of the particular facts in the world, and the single principle we seek must be one that can show itself to be the origin of mind as of all else, and to be manifested in mind as it is in nature ; but mind is above all else purposive—and so the one principle to which all is preferred must to be such as to be at once the origin and the satisfaction of purpose.

' Science aims at explaining the world—and must always remember that mind is not only one of the facts in the world, but is the ruling principle of existence itself ; so the world can only be explained by the demonstration of its essentially spiritual character.' N. pp. 14f.

' The real cause of a thing's being what it is, is to be sought not in the past but rather in the future. Man is not what he is only because he was once an ape, but he was both apish and is human in order that he may hereafter be divine. The world is not what it is because it was once part of the nebula, but because it is ultimately to become the Kingdom of Heaven. Society may be historically the offspring of sexual passion, and religion of the vilest super-stition, but that does not touch the validity of either.

' Here then is the real unity and permanence that science seeks—in the Eternal Mind, in Whose consciousness all space and all time are comprehended, and in His unalterable purpose which is the sole reality in man or in the world, the sole universal law, the only true uniformity of nature. We may indeed take any particular causal series by itself and see that it is truly necessary. But that whole *series* can only come into being in order that the one Eternal Purpose might be realised in it. The only point in which nature is truly uniform is to be found in the fact that the whole creation groaneth and travaileth together, waiting for the fruition of the divine blessedness." N. p. 21.

That paper, written by an undergraduate more than forty years ago, is still fresh and interesting, and its criticism of some scientists is still relevant. It was a subject which always interested him, and he returned to it again and again. In 1911, as the exceptionally young headmaster of Repton, he read a paper on *Scientific Ideas among the Ancient Greeks* to the School Scientific Society. Here is one passage from it :

' Modern science tends to concentrate on the efficient cause and always ignores the final cause. There is no harm in that if it knows what it is about. But it is substituting history for explanation, and it must not afterwards pretend that history is explanation, though of course there can be no explanation without it.' S. p. 16.

Twenty years later he contributed to *Essays and Studies* by Members of the English Association, vol. xvii (second series), Oxford, 1932, a characteristic paper on ' Poetry and Science.' Here is one passage from it :

' Copernicus and Galileo adopted the . . . hypothesis that the sun is the centre, at least of that system to which our planet primarily belongs ; and I believe that scientists are agreed in saying that the only reason for preferring the heliocentric astronomy is that it is simpler. The courageous (to use no more offensive term), dogmatism of those who assure us in defiance of the plain evidence of our senses, that the earth does really go round the sun, when everybody can see the sun going round the earth, for no other reason than that it makes their calculating simpler, leaves the mere theologian gasping.' T. pp. 9, 10.

Just before he wrote the paper for *Essays and Studies*, the Archbishop referred to the limitations of natural science in an address he gave to the York Diocesan Conference ;

' I think it is possible to get people to see that without any disparagement whatever of the immense service, theoretical and practical, which science has brought us, its methods do not cover the whole of life. Kepler is reported to have had an unfortunate experience in his first marriage and to have decided for his second to proceed on scientific lines. So he analysed all his female acquaintances and their qualities, and selected the one in whose case there was the greatest preponderance of merits over defects ; and the result was that the second marriage was worse than the first, whereupon he pronounced the problem insoluble by human reason. And so it is, if by reason you mean analytic ratiocination. But it is unreasonable to suppose that reason is limited to that process, or that an intuitive process is not every bit as reasonable as any amount of mental calculation.' F. July, 1932.

While he was at York the Archbishop let out a very alert and voracious cat to flutter all sorts of academic dovecotes, particularly in the modern universities of the North of England, by writing an article in the *York Quarterly* in which he said that while religious people had been occupied about the rights and wrongs of Denominational Education, there had been developing in ever more *menacing* proportions a peril far greater than any Undenominationalism could ever be, *the peril of a purely scientific education.* This made people sit up and take notice, if only because the typical modern journalist and author have taken for granted that the need of our national education is science, and yet more science. Quotations will make clear the argument of the Archbishop's article :

' The recent increase in the number of secondary schools in the country is a source of gratification to all who care for educational progress. We still have much leeway to make up. But it is seldom realised how completely the scientific side of these schools preponderates as against the literary ; nor is the effect of this preponderance upon the pupils often appreciated. We are training a generation expert in certain departments of science, but utterly un-developed in imagination, in sympathy, in social and political instinct, in moral discrimination. It is easy, especially in the new urban universities, to find many men, and no small number of women, who are really able, taking high honours in their science examinations, but are mentally puerile so soon as questions involving value— moral, social, aesthetic—are brought into discussion. Their technical attainments will secure for them positions of influence and leadership in industrial and other fields ; but they will not be qualified to use those positions to the best advantage either of the people with whom they are specially concerned or of the country as a whole. . . .

' We need an education which shall enable us to under-stand and act wisely in relation to our environment. Leav-ing aside for the moment things divine, the most important part of our environment consists neither of planets nor of chemicals, but of human beings. No doubt the wisdom that we need in our dealings with them is mainly won by the experience of social life. That is why the fundamental element in a school is not the instruction given in class rooms, but the life of the school as a society of young people. But it is also true that, while sharing in such a life develops the social instincts, the development of the mind in relation to human beings, their needs and problems, comes by study of what are called the humanities : the great movements of mankind, their achievements and failures, in History ; their loftiest aspirations and deepest feelings, in Literature. An education which does not give great place to one or both of these, is dangerously un-balanced.' E.

'Mathematics and Science are not only of incalculable value in their utility for life, but are among the noblest disciplines of mind and soul. It is not the study of these great subjects, but the almost exclusive study of them by so many of the rising generation that gives ground for alarm. This exclusive attention is bad for citizenship, but is still worse for religion. It creates a type of mind which is clumsy and blundering in relation to all questions of Value—of Beauty and Ugliness in nature, art or conduct ; of Right and Wrong in all their less obvious manifestations. It creates a tendency to deal with men in the mass, by generalisations, rather than as individuals. Marxianism is, I believe, bad science ; but half its viciousness consists in its attempt to treat the problems of human life on purely scientific lines. An exclusively scientific training leads men to demand crucial experiments with spiritual force such as are familiar in physical or chemical laboratories, forgetting that those forces can only be apprehended by the intui-tions that are born of loyalty and sympathy. Religion has its close affinities with Science, for it depends on the veritable truth of its convictions ; and Science is an invaluable purge of Religion, cleansing it of illusion and superstition. But the actual life of Religion is far nearer to Art than to Science, and nearer still to human relationships.' E.

In 1943 the Archbishop delivered the Beckly Lecture, and this was published under the title, *Social Witness and Evangelism*. There was an appendix to this, *Evangelism in the Modern World*, in which he returned again to this subject of the limitations of natural science, particularly as the main factor in education :

'The serious difficulty is the absence from the mind of those whom we would address of the ideas we wish to utilize, and the presence there of other ideas which are incompatible with these. . . . The frame of mind about which I am speaking has two main features, both due to the undue prominence of the physical sciences in our recent thinking and education. One is the tendency to suppose that only what can be measured or weighed is really knowable or indeed apprehensible by the mind at all ; the other is the spectator attitude.' U. p. 27.

' This spectator attitude is proper and, indeed, necessary in a laboratory ; there emotional reactions will seriously distort the apprehension of truth. It is quite inappropriate in human relationships and in religion. Our education is in a fair way to hand over human relationships to passion divorced from thought, and to make religion a mere matter of personal opinion or feeling or both, but *not* the total self-committal of man to God which alone is true religion.' U. p. 28.

THEISM

In course of time, finite minds appeared in the world that astronomical physics describes. Dr. Temple emphasised the fact that these minds are not mere episodes in the process, determined by material events ; they are in some sense free, and self-determined. A man can choose what he will think about. Any explanation of the process which is to be satisfactory must, then, explain the appearance of minds within it. Obviously, a cause must be adequate to its presumed effects. But, seeking for an explanation, a mind will never stop short with a cause. It will always ask for the cause of that cause, and so on *ad infinitum.*

' The goal of the intellect is the apprehension of the whole universe as a nexus of relations. No doubt the ideal is unattainable by a human mind within the period of a human life on this planet ; but it cannot be unattainable in principle. . . . But at present the temporal character is not altogether overcome. For while we are still at the intellectual or scientific stage, the mind is characterised by unrest and motion. This is the essence of " intellection " or science, that it asks " Why " perpetually ; as soon as it is answered, it asks " Why ? " again.' L. pp. 71, 72.

' But if from some other department of Mind's activity an answer is suggested, the intellect (if not impeded by " intellectualist " dogmatism) will gladly accept it. And Mind does accept as final an explanation in terms of Purpose and Will ; for this (and, so far as our experience goes, this alone) combines efficient and final causation. " Why is this canvas covered with paint ? "   " Because I painted it."   " Why did you do that ? "   " Because I hoped to create a thing of beauty for the delight of myself and others." If, then, we find any ground for saying that the world is the product of an Infinite Will, created for the sake of its Value (the Problem of Evil is here crying out for attention, as in John i. 3. But, like St. John, we ignore it for the present), the intellect, which could not *from any consideration of its own procedure* reach any such result, will none the less accept this doctrine as altogether agreeable to itself.' L. p. 89.

In each field of experience the mind finds its own nature in the object. But it finds Mind on such a scale as to feel the object more wholly other even than when it seemed strange and alien. The intellectual experience, and the æsthetic experience also, when they are examined, have religious implications.

' It is wonder that prompts the mind to examine its environment—and at first the elementary wonder how to make the best of it ; but the enquiry ends in the wonder of awe, before that which, the more it is understood, by so much the more transcends our understanding. " In wonder, says Aristotle, does philosophy begin ; and in astonishment, says Plato, does all true philosophy finish " (Coleridge). For what manner of mind is that of which our science forms but an inkling in its analysis and systematisation of the experienced world ? From the play of minutest particles to the sweep of stars in their courses, the work of Mind is found—of a Mind so mighty in range and scope, so sure in adjustment of infinitesimal detail, that before it all our science is clumsy and precarious. Nothing merely strange or alien can seem so incomparably transcendent as that Mind in the likeness of which our own minds are fashioned yet before which they can only confess their impotence.

' The search for Beauty leads to the same conclusion as the search for Truth. The artist is ever essaying to depict a human form more beautiful than any actual human form can ever be, a landscape lit with an illumination such as never was seen by mortal eye :

' The light that never was by sea or land,
The consecration and the poets' dream.

' Yet this is no emanation from the artist's brain ; it is rather the attempt to catch and fix that Beauty of Reality, of which all beautiful things are momentary and partial manifestations. This true Beauty is apprehended, as it were, in fitful visions ; but when apprehended, it is not as dream or hallucination, but as most real fact. Many artists have spoken of it—it suffices to refer to Shelley's *Hymn to Intellectual Beauty* . . . ; all artists have won some glimpse of it, and thereafter sought it diligently.

' Just in the degree in which the artist—be his medium what it may—succeeds in winning from us that concentration of attention which is the essential condition of æsthetic experience, he makes a claim implicitly to satisfy the human soul. The beautiful object claims and holds our minds as nothing is entitled to claim and hold them which has not the promise at least of that which saints have called the Beatific Vision. In the moment of deep appreciation, all movement of thought is checked ; in place of the movement of thought there is the activity of receptive rest ; in place of the apprehended movement of time there is

The moment eternal, just that and no more,
When ecstasy's utmost we catch at the core.
for in that moment Beauty, whether of nature or of art,
Here, for the sight of mortal man, has given
To one brief moment caught from fleeting time
The appropriate calm of blest eternity.' M. pp. 156, 157.
The same thing is true of the experience of moral obliga-
tion. All ethical judgment has an absolute quality ; this
also implies personal relation, which means faith in God.

' Moral value resides not in acts or actions, but in a
certain type of character—the righteous character. This
is the character which subordinates all other considerations
to the claims of the community of persons. But because
it is of persons, the highest interest of the community and
its members is a personal interest, the fulfilment of being as
Persons ; and this is Righteousness. Plato speaks with the
authentic voice of morality when he complains that those
who had great repute as statesmen had " filled the city full
of harbours and docks and walls and revenues and such
trifles to the exclusion of temperance and righteousness."
For whatever is a truly personal good—a good which
resides in a person—takes priority over all non-personal
goods, because morality is the discovery or recognition by
persons of personality in others, to whom by the common
attribute of personality they are bound in the ties of community membership. What most concerns this is, therefore,
the highest good. That is why moral considerations must
take precedence of æsthetic, if the two conflict. The essential
condition of Value is the discovery by mind of itself in its
other ; this is only perfectly accomplished when the other
is itself a living mind or person.' M. p. 193.

' If we anticipate the results of future discussions we can
offer this summary of moral obligations : Your being is
personal ; love as a person in fellow-membership with all
others who, being personal, are your fellow-members
in the community of persons. Strive to grow in fullness

of personality, in width and depth of fellowship ; and seek to draw the energy for this from that to which you and all things owe their origin, the Personal Love which is Creator and Sustainer of the World.' M. p. 196.

Not in Whitehead's principle of organism but in personality is the clue to the source and meaning of the universe.

' The real enemy to-day is not materialism ; materialism as a philosophy is as dead as a doornail. The real enemy is a spiritual interpretation of the Universe which gives a place to the supreme values of the spiritual life—beauty, goodness and truth—but which does not give full value to the fact of Personality.' Ab. p. 173.

' The goal of Science is not reached ;   Science only exists in departmental fragments :   physics, chemistry, biology, and the rest. The goal of art is not reached : there is no experience obtainable through the æsthetic faculties in which the soul can find satisfaction for ever. The goal of Ethics is not reached : it would be realised in the pursuit of a purpose lofty enough to claim the allegiance of all our faculties and rich enough to exercise them all, conducted in a fellowship bound together by ties of mutual love ; but man cannot evolve out of himself that purpose, nor can he of himself create that fellowship. All of these efforts of Mind in its search for satisfaction demand the actuality of an ideal to which they point but which they never reach. Ethics suggests a Will which is perfectly self-determined, and yet is active altogether in love ; such a Will, if it be made manifest, will satisfy the aspirations of Art, for its manifestation will claim and deserve eternal contemplation ; such a Will, if it control the Universe, is the very principle of unity which Science seeks, for Will, while remaining constant in its Purpose, chooses now this, now that, as means to its end, and is the only principle which, self-explanatory in itself, explains what it orders or informs. Is there such a Will ? Only if there is, can the Universe be deemed rational ; Man's creative mind can find satisfaction only if there be a Divine Creative Mind with which it may have communion.' L. p. 258.

It is interesting to compare with this a vivid account of the theistic interpretation of life in *The Church Looks Forward*, in a broadcast address on ' The Crisis of Western Civilisation ' which, the Archbishop himself said, strikes the key note of that great book :

' The Christian tradition of Western Europe, and consequently also of the Western World . . . rests on certain postulates which are indispensable but are often ignored. The first is the essential unity of the whole created order— or, if you like, of nature, including human nature. Man may be more than a part of nature, but he is that. At every turn he is dependent on his natural environment, and if he is to prosper in the long run it must be as a partner with nature in the production and utilisation of its resources, not as its lord exploiting nature for his own ends ; that way leads to sterilisation and death. This partnership with nature did not have to be emphasised in earlier times because it was so evident and was everywhere taken for granted. It is the invention of machinery which has seemed to set a division between man and nature, making him appear to be at once its master and relatively independent of it. That is, of course, an illusory appearance ; but it is one to which modern civilisation gives rise, and which it is now necessary, as it was not necessary in former times, explicitly to expose. Man, in the Christian as in the scientific view, is part of nature, having his own place in the one great scheme, which is the plan and purpose of the Creator.

' But, secondly, that place is a special one ; for while on the side of his bodily life man belongs to nature, he alone among created things has the capacity and the need to choose the objects for which his strength shall be expended. We all recognise this difference. As G. K. Chesterton used to say, " No one asks a puppy what kind of dog it means to be when it grows up." This is the essential difference. Other animals have that element in reason which is called intelligence at least in some degree ; they think out means to the ends which their specific nature prompts them to pursue. They do not choose what ends they shall pursue ; man does ; and it is in this choice of ends that he becomes morally responsible and capable of fellowship with God. His chief end is " to glorify God and enjoy Him for ever."

' This involves the third postulate—that man, who on one side is part of nature and is as such a creature of a few years, is capable of and destined for fellowship with the eternal God. Consequently his choice of ends—his choice between good and evil—not only has consequences for his neighbours or for the society of which he is a member, but has eternal significance for himself and even for God. He and his conduct have, therefore, an importance which is far more than biological or social or political. He has an infinite value because God loves him—not because of any quality of his own part from his relationship to God, but because God loves him. And this is the basis of his claim to freedom—his claim to be himself, to live his own life and fulfil his own destiny. This also is the ground of the primacy of justice among social and civic virtues. If I am a creature with a life-span of sixty or seventy years, I cannot count for anything over against the nation or the State. But if I am a child of God, destined for eternal fellowship with Him, I have therein a dignity with which the State can make no comparable claim. It is here that man's dignity resides, in a region where all are equal. In the English Coronation Service the King is seated as the token of earthly royalty is placed upon his head ; but he is kneeling when just afterwards he receives the effectual tokens of divine grace in the same manner in which any labourer in any village church receives them. At the point where alone man has true dignity he is completely equal to all his fellow men ; his infinite value is of such a kind as to shut out all superiority.

' So this which is the source of man's claim to freedom and to justice is the source also of democracy. This may take many social and political forms ; but the heart of it is always trust in the ordinary man—and the test of it is not whether the majority prevails but whether the minority is given freedom to express itself and to become the majority if it can.' Ae. pp. 79–81.

He took the personality of God very seriously, as is shown by his treatment of the notions of immanence and transcendence. A purpose or principle may be immanent in a process, he taught, but in relation to a process a person is always transcendent. God is immament in the world as man is immanent in his conduct—as ' a principle of vari-ability,' but He is Himself transcendent and unchangeable, the eternally self-identical, the I AM. William Temple took the Divine personality more seriously than most philosophers have done.

' I know that His nature transcends all categories appre-hended by the human mind ; but though that warns us to maintain a reverent agnosticism in many directions, it also assures us that we shall speak of Him most adequately when we use the highest categories that we have. It is, therefore, better to call Him " personal " with the necessary reservations than to call Him non-personal, because this, to us, is in effect to think of Him as less than personal. If it is misleading to use with reference to God the pronoun " He," it is still more misleading to use the pronoun " It." ' Ag.

' The actual practice of religion in any of its forms admits men to experience of the personal action of God in many degrees of self-disclosure. This field has not been worked over by scientific students of the subject with the diligence which it deserves. That is natural enough, because precise and critical observation is very difficult and experiment is from the nature of the case impossible. What is very startling to the philosopher, whose mental habit is controlled by scientific interests, is the abundance of testimony given by those who have had intimate experience of men's spiritual life to the conviction that in the early stages prayer receives literal fulfilment with great frequency ; that later on this becomes less frequent, until it seems almost to cease, as though God at first gives encouragement of the most obvious kind and later withdraws this in order to evoke a deeper trust. Such theories call for scientific investigation ; the evidence should be weighed and tested. But if this very common assertion of the persons best qualified to know is well founded, it indicates not only a power but a readiness to practise with much freedom that adaption to circumstances which we have asserted as a necessary inference from the Personality of God.' M. p. 297. He told me that the people mostly in his mind were Père Grou and St. Francis de Sales.

MIRACLE

This thoroughgoing belief in Divine Personality led him to an interesting and stimulating philosophy of miracle. This was stated clearly in *Christus Veritas:*

' Purpose exhibits its own unity in the adaptations to changing conditions of which it is capable. We should therefore antecedently expect, what religious experience is found to affirm, that God not only controls all the world by the laws of its own being, inherent in its elements by His creative act, but that as He made it for the realisation f certain values, so in pursuit of those values He acts directly upon its course as occasion in His all-seeing judgment may require.' O. p. 100.

The relation of this to natural science and the philosophy of nature is set out explicitly in the Gifford Lectures, where he says that the dichotomy of events into normal and miraculous is wholly unphilosophic.

' The naive religious view is that God made the world and imposed laws upon it, which it invariably observes unless He intervenes to modify the operation of His own laws. From this naive view springs the suggestion that it would better comport with the infinite majesty of God that He should from the outset impose such laws as would never stand in need of modification. But if, as we have seen ground for holding, the World-Process is itself the medium of God's personal action, the whole situation is altered. There is nothing majestic about invariable constancy of personal action, which remains unaltered whether the circumstances are the same or not ; rather should it be called mulish. Constancy of purpose is a noble characteristic, but it shows itself, not in unalterable uniformity of conduct, but in perpetual self-adaptation, with an infinite delicacy of graduation, to different circumstances, so that, however these may vary, the one unchanging purpose is always served.

If we adopt this view we shall have also to hold that no Law of Nature as discovered by physical science is ultimate. It is a general statement of that course of conduct in Nature which is sustained by the purposive action of God so long and so far as it will serve His purpose. No doubt it is true that the same cause will always produce the same effect in the same circumstances. Our contention is that an element in every actual cause, and indeed the determinant element, is the active purpose of God fulfilling itself with that perfect constancy which calls for an infinite graduation of adjustments in the process. Where any adjustment is so considerable as to attract notice it is called a miracle ; but it is not a specimen of a class, it is an illustration of the general character of the World-Process.' M. p. 267.

The following quotation explains the connection of miracle with revelation :

' Our enquiry did not lead us to the bare assertion that the world owes its origin and continuous existence to the Divine Will, but also to the consequent conviction that all things are in their measure an expression of that Will which sustains, but also moulds and guides all things, so that the unity of the world, its principle of rational coherence, is the Divine Personality in self-expression. (This is the conviction which finds expression in St. John i. 1–3 and Colossians i. 17.) Further, we were brought to the view that, because the world's principle of unity is personal, its manifestation will not be through invariable uniformity, but in such variability of adaptation as expresses the constancy of the divine character in face of the various moments of universal history. For the most part we shall expect to find, as we find in fact, a widespread uniformity ; because where there is no special and sufficient occasion for variation, its occurrence would argue caprice rather than constancy. Moreover, we have seen that, so far as the moral quality of human life is matter of concern to the Creator, it supplies a reason not so much for variation to meet special contingencies as for a uniformity sufficiently general to be the basis of purposive action. But where there is sufficient occasion, the creative will may vary its more usual activity ; when this occurs it is not through the intrusion of some normally inoperative cause, but through the action of what alone accounts for all existences and occurrences, the volition of personal Deity. It is thus chacteristic of God that He should usually act by what to us is uniformity (though the appearance even of this may conceal variations too delicate for our perception and too small to affect our confidence in action), just as it is characteristic of Him to vary His action when the occasion is sufficient. Yet there is inevitably a peculiarly revealing quality in the occasional variations, both because they show what occasions are in the divine judgment sufficient, and because they are the issue of a specially directed activity in face of the sufficient occasion, whereas the general uniformity obviously does not issue from such specially directed activity. That God did not intervene in answer to my prayer to save the life of some friend during the Great War by deflection of a bullet may perhaps be indirectly a manifestation of His love both for my friend and for me ; but if He raised Jesus of Nazareth from death, that is a much more direct manifestation of His relationship to the Life and Death of Jesus.' M. pp. 301–303.

And this last quotation contains the answer to an increasingly common objection to miracles :

' The massive impressiveness of nature's apparent uniformity leads some religious students of natural science to suppose that it is more consonant with Divine Majesty to impose on nature one order never to be varied than to meet successive situations with appropriately varied activity. We have already commented on this view, which seems to make the Divine Will more external to the natural order than the course of our argument would suggest, and also ignores the fact that personal wisdom is not shown in rigid uniformity of behaviour, but in constancy of purpose expressed through infinitely various response to different conditions.' M. p. 307.

CREATION

The assertion of the personality of God is another way of stating the Christian doctrine of Creation. The universe owes its existence to the will of God :

' We can make no truce with any suggestion that the world for the most part goes by itself on its own way while God intervenes now and again with an act of His own. The course of thought, which enables us to hold together religious faith in the living God and the picture of the world with which science provides us, renders the whole notion of such divine intrusion from without intolerable and incredible ; for this course of thought has perpetually recurred to the insistence that all occurrences find their ultimate ground in the Divine Volition. But if we stopped here we should only have affirmed that in the entire course of cosmic history is to be found the self-revelation of God ; and that, no doubt, is true ; but as no man can ever hope to contemplate that history in its entirety, it cannot be said to afford a revelation to us or for us.' M. p. 304.

But just in so far as we take seriously the idea of Divine personality we shall expect some experiences to reveal God more significantly than others :

' If there is ground for holding that such agents (free or partially free) exist, then we must expect to find instances of divine action relevant to the situations which their free acts create, and while such action will be no more divine than the constant purpose which sustain all things in being, it will have a specially revelatory quality, because it is an expression of the divine character in face of critical situations, and not only an episode in the age-long energy of God.' M. pp. 304, 505.

REVELATION

Because personality reveals itself particularly in dealing with persons as persons we shall expect to find divine revelation rather in human history and personal experience than in nature :

' If man is spiritual and the stars are not, then God is vastly more concerned about the selfishness of a little child than about the wreck of a solar system.' O. p. 96.

The personal God can be revealed only to and in and through persons :

' The whole Truth of God could not find expression in a human life, but the perfection of intellectual virtue (i.e., the readiness of the mind to apprehend rightly whatever it may have the opportunity to apprehend) can do so ; the whole of apprehensible Beauty could not be concentrated in one human consciousness, though perfect Beauty of many kinds and graces can be realised there ; the whole Goodness of God can in its completeness be expressed in a human life. We do not now discuss what conditions are requisite for this to happen ; we are only concerned at present to assert its possibility in principle.' O. p. 31.

' In personality as we know it in ourselves, the process of evolution has produced a being capable of apprehending universal truth and absolute obligation ; for though our range in these regards may be limited, yet in principle we are familiar with such apprehensions. The truth that $2 + 2 = 4$ is not dependent on circumstances ; it is genuinely universal. But beyond the universal and the absolute it is self-evidently impossible to go. Man then, in respect of his reason and conscience, is akin to whatever is ultimate. Here is the image of God stamped on human nature. Here also is the condition making possible a personal revelation of God in human nature. The Incarnation is in principle possible.' Z. pp. 30, 31.

Nevertheless, revelation in and through persons must be distorted by any defect in the persons through whom it comes :

' The revelation given in the majesty of the starry heavens may be perfect in its kind, though its kind is markedly inadequate ; the revelation given through the reason and conscience of men is more adequate in kind, but in that kind is usually imperfect. . . . The existence of evil in its worst form, that of sin, introduces a defect, and it may be a distortion, into all revelation given through the medium of human personality, unless there be found an instance of this which is free from sin. This defect or distortion is something more than limitation in fullness or complete-

ness ; it affects the quality of the revelation in ways that
are not capable of ascertainment in advance ; and this fact
must be borne in mind in any attempt to set forth the
general conditions of the possibility of revelation.'   M.
p. 306.

The mode of this revelation is not in infallibly authentic-
ated information :

'(The earlier and supposedly preparatory revelation)
consisted primarily in historical events, and secondarily
in the illumination of the minds of prophets to read those
events as disclosing the judgment or the purpose of God.
What we find in the Old Testament Scriptures is not mainly,
if at all, authoritative declaration of theological doctrine,
but living apprehension of a living process wherein those
whose minds are enlightened by divine communion can
discern in part the purposive activity of God.

'Revelation so conceived is the full actuality of that
relationship between Nature, Man and God, which throughout these Lectures we are seeking to articulate. First there
is the world-process, which in its more complex compon-
ents, if not throughout, is organic in principle ; secondly,
we have the fact that certain organisms, to wit ourselves,
occurring as episodes of the world-process, are able to
apprehend and in part to comprehend that process ;
thirdly, we infer from this that the process, in order to give
rise to such episodes in its course, must be regarded as
itself grounded in a mental principle ; fourthly, enquiry
into that interaction of the intelligent organism with its
environment, which we call thought, compels the assertion that the principle in which the world-process is
grounded, is not only mental but spiritual and personal ;
fifthly, this leads us to the conviction that the process itself
and all occurrences within it—including the intelligences
of men—are due to the purposive action of that Person
whose reality has been established as the governing fact
of existence. *He guides the process ; He guides the minds*

of men ; the interaction of the process and the minds which are alike guided by Him is the essence of revelation. . . .

'While the apparently uniform process of the world is, in its measure, a revelation of God for those whose minds are alert to its significance, it is less fully revelatory than specially adapted activities for the meeting of such contingencies as give sufficient ground for such activities. It is, therefore, not unnatural or inappropriate that the term Revelation should be commonly used with a special reference to these occasions. But these must be understood as particular and conspicuous illustrations of the principle of revelation already stated—the interaction of the world-process and the minds, both being alike guided by God. In these events too—be it a deliverance of a nation from bondage in despite of all calculable probabilities, be it the Incarnation in a human life of that Self-Utterance of God which is the ground of the created universe—there is no imparting of truth as the intellect apprehends truth, but there is event and appreciation ; and in the coincidence of these the revelation consists. . . .

'*From all this it follows that there is no such thing as revealed truth. There are truths of revelation, that is to say, propositions which express the results of correct thinking concerning revelation ; but they are not themselves directly revealed.*' M. pp. 312–17.

But, in addition to revelation in objective facts, and in minds divinely illuminated to appreciate the facts, there is some direct self-communication from God to the soul :

'It would be strange if He acted only in the inorganic and non-spiritual, and dealt with spirits akin to Himself only by the indirect testimony of the rest of His creation. . . . The signal instance of a conviction that must be credited to a divine self-communication given by means of such intercourse is the prophetic faith in the righteousness and holiness of God, of which the intellectual formula is Ethical Monotheism. This was certainly not an inference from experience ; it was an illumination arising from communion with God in the activity of conscience and in adoration, in the light of which the prophets read the history of their times. Even so, it was not a communicated " faith," but a crystallisation of thought and feeling under pressure of facts experienced or anticipated, as when Abraham exclaimed, " Shall not the Judge of all the earth do right ? " ' M. p. 318.

Faith, then, is not the holding of correct doctrines, but personal fellowship with the living God :

' Correct doctrine will both express this, assist it and issue from it ; incorrect doctrine will misrepresent this and hinder or prevent it. Doctrine is of an importance too great to be exaggerated, but its place is secondary not primary. I do not believe in any creed, but I use certain creeds to express, to conserve, and to deepen my faith in God. *What is offered to man's apprehension in any specific Revelation is not truth concerning God, but the living God Himself. . . .*

' The question still remains—by what means does the revelation authenticate itself ? From the nature of the case it must offer its own credentials ; that revelation should have to appeal to anything beside itself to establish its character as revelation, would be patent absurdity. The older tradition found the authentication in miracle and fulfilled prediction. God, being the supreme power in the universe, was held to give evidence of His special activity in it by setting aside its normal process and accomplishing some transformation by His creative fiat. So Moses was to convince his people of the authenticity of his mission by the conversion of his staff into a snake. Whether God ever does such things in accommodation to primitive minds is not a question for Natural Theology ; if He could want to do it, He could also do it ; but the probable explanation of this and similar episodes is to be sought in hypnotism. At a more developed stage there arises a demand for fitness in the sign offered, and some coherence with the spiritual content of the revelation. I could not expect my hearers to be any the more ready to accept my philosophy if I were able before their eyes to turn my pen into a stick of sealing-wax (Cf. Matthew Arnold, *Literature and Dogma*, p. 49). So it is also with fulfilled prediction. Great attention has been given, for example, to the close resemblance between the details of Psalm xxii and those of the story of Our Lord's Passion, but this is a false line of argument ; not by any irrelevant thaumaturgy in either the physical or the psychological realm does the Lord God Almighty make His presence known. Yet when we turn from essentially trifling details to broad principles, the old attention to miracle and prophecy is seen to be justified. The evidence of God's special activity is indeed not to be found in what baffles the intelligence, but rather in power active for such purposes as may reasonably be supposed divine. Where power and mercy are combined, there is God manifest ; where we see righteousness or love, we see the character of God ; where we see these triumphing we see God in action ; where we see them achieve their purpose despite all calculable probabilities, there we acknowledge God signally self-revealed. We do not know that it costs Him more (to speak humanly), to work the most startling so-called miracle, than to maintain the habitual motion of the planets ; but where that happens which former experience leads us to expect, we are less impelled to ponder on the divine nature as therein disclosed, than when our expectation is negatived by an exhibition of that character in ways unpredictable by us. All is of God, but not all things equally display His character, and not all things equally call our attention to His character as displayed.

' So too with prophecy : if God makes Himself known we shall expect to find progress in man's apprehension of Him, and even in that which He discloses. But if He is

active in the progress, the progress must bear the marks
of His continuing guidance ; its earlier stages must be
incomplete, and one condition of advance is that men
become aware of the incompleteness of what they have.
So the earlier look forward to the later, groping after it,
adumbrating it. Some parts of the adumbration will be
mistaken, arising from the human limitations of the prophet
or seer ; but some parts will be filled in or completed, being
gleams of the light that lighteth every man, which, if it
ever shines in full brilliance, must be recognisably their
completion. This continuity of development along constant and converging lines is evidence of a continuing
illumination ; and if in some event the converging lines
of development meet and all find their fulfilment, that
is corroborative evidence of authentic revelation alike in
the preparatory and in the culminating stages.

' These, then, are the marks of a true revelation, of which
we have already described the necessary mode : a union of
holiness and power, before which our spirits bow in awe,
and which authenticates itself by continuous development
to some focal point in which all preparatory revelation
finds fulfilment, and from which illumination radiates into
every department of life and being. Whatever claims to
be revelation makes good that claim in the degree in which
it approximates to the ideal thus described.' M. pp. 323–325.

' The man of faith did not reach his faith by scientific
inference. By training or by nature or by both he has
been led to fellowship with God, and has found therein
an experience which both vindicates itself (Cf. 1 John v. 10),
and throws light on all other experiences whatsoever. The
central element in Christianity is not a doctrine about God,
but is God Himself active in the Incarnate Word. Faith is
not a conclusion but a starting-point ; reasoning will
enrich its content, but that new content when incorporated
into the apprehension of Faith becomes a fresh starting-
point for thought and practice. God is for faith not an

inference, but a *datum*—and that in the most literal sense, for if we have faith in Him it is because He has given Himself to us.' Ai. pp. 6, 7.

RELIGIOUS EXPERIENCE

Religious experience is the human side, the Divine side is revelation, of the communion or fellowship between God and man :

' Men seek God by the way of Knowledge ; but at the end of the road they have only formed a conception of Him ; they have not met with Him. Men seek God by the way of Beauty ; but at the end they have not found Him ; they have only formed a yearning which no beauty on earth can satisfy. Men seek God by the way of Conduct ; but they only find a Law from which they infer a Lawgiver ; God is still hidden. If we begin without God and try to find a way to Him, we shall at best reach a vague Pantheism, which will only satisfy if we read into it a personal interpretation for which in strict logic it has no room. That is, indeed, what many people do ; having some real religious experience but not recognising it for what it is, they suppose that they have begun without God and have also ended to their full satisfaction without God, when as a matter of fact they have been with Him all along.' K. pp. 68, 69.

Our knowledge of God may grow, our experience of Him may develop, but He is unchanging, the self-identical, the I AM.

' No man of any spiritual experience would be prepared to tolerate the suggestion . . . that when we set out to worship, we have first to determine the precise degree of perfection which God has now attained in order that we may nicely adapt our praises. We know that the God before whom we humble ourselves is the God to whom Abraham spoke, if Abraham existed as an individual, which after all does not very much matter. Our knowledge of Him ought to be quite different from Abraham's, for we have received the illumination which was given to the world in Jesus Christ ; but it is the same God with whom we are entering into communion. If it is not, then all the experience which seems to the religious man to be Divine fellowship is an illusion from top to bottom. Religion can never rest on the historical method. It will use it to illuminate the true contents of its own traditions. It will use it in order to know more fully the way by which God, in His mercy, has met the weakness of human nature from stage to stage, always leading steadily on to a fuller truth. But the religious man will never be content with the belief that there is no unchanging and eternal God, and nothing at all except the changing state of human consciousness from generation to generation. If that turned out to be true, we should have to accept it, but in accepting it we should be laying religion once and for ever on one side.' P. p. 20.

' If the general argument of philosophy seemed to me to incline towards atheism, I could not confidently reject the theory of some psychologists that all religious experience is illusion. If there were no experience which seemed to be a personal relationship with God, I should have to admit that the balance of probability in the general philosophic argument is not decisive. But the two converge and support each other ; it is in the mutual support of general argument and religious experience that we find the main strength of the case for theism.' Z. p. 30.

' Science, Art and Morals seem to require for their own completion, and for their unity with one another, the existence of God ; and there are men in almost every part of the world and almost every period of history who believe themselves to have had direct experience of communion with God. Religious experience, therefore, confirms and is confirmed by the whole tendency of philosophy.' L. p. 259.

'The objection is usually based on the supposition that some men have no religious experience at all. But this is very doubtful and seems even to be false. There are many men who pay little attention to their religious experience, and in whom (often for that reason) it is rudimentary; there are many who do not recognise it for what it is. But it is doubtful if any man can go through life without ever feeling reverence for something which is morally so high above him as to be out of his reach, or awe before the great Reality on which he is utterly dependent. And it may safely be said that no one escapes, though he may to his own satisfaction explain away, the sense of absolute obligation. All of these are in their true nature religious experiences—the recognition of an Absolute. To understand them fully will, of itself, carry a man far into theology. If his reverence and his awe are justified, they imply a Reality fit to be their occasion. If he is genuinely subject to the obligation, that implies a universe in which obligation has a place. Of all the various forms of undeveloped or unsophisticated religious experience, this sense of absolute obligation is the most certainly universal and the most commonly recognised. It is on this, therefore, that our argument will chiefly rest.

'The absolute obligation due to the absolute Value of Truth and Beauty is a command of God and a means of access to Him ; but it is in the claims of Goodness that this command is most universally found and the access to God most fully effected. . . . Goodness comes first because we are men, and Goodness is the Value which is actualised by men alone, and is, therefore, the specific human value ; thus it is the Truth or Reality of man, and may be described as Truth expressed, and so made beautiful, in human life.' O. pp. 39, 40.

The distinction sometimes drawn or attempted between authority and experience or ' spirit ' is false :

' Consciousness of authority and submission to it is the

very heart of true religion. It is because of this that religious history is so full of tragic submission to authority of the wrong kind, and of consequent reactions in which men try to practise religion apart from authority and fall into every variety of phantasy. The heart of religion, as has already been emphasised, is acknowledgement by the finite of insignificance before the Infinite, by the sinner of pollution before the Holy, by the creature of total dependence before the Creator. It is in its essence a submission to authority.' M. p. 343.

For the individual, his religious experience is largely determined by his belief, that is, by tradition. But in religious history as a whole, belief and tradition are moulded by experience. All spiritual authority—the authority of God and of His self-revelation, for example—works through the free appreciation and acceptance of those who yield to it. It is because God is perfectly good and is adored as such, not because He is omnipotent and is feared as such, that He has spiritual authority over me.

FREEDOM AND GRACE

This raises, for Christian theism, the problem of human freedom and the relation to it of divine grace. How does God control or help man, while acting through and not against his freedom, and what does man need which only God can supply ? Dr. Temple found the answer in the denial of all human freedom over against God and the affirmation of complete human freedom in submission to God. Men's freedom is real, but it is not enough :

' They are free, for the origin of their actions is themselves ; they are bound hand and foot, for from themselves there is no flight.' L. p. 144.

It is the freedom which is perfect bondage. It is obvious that man can never *will* to become completely unselfish while he is still selfish. He can never escape from self-centredness by his own effort—to do so would be to stand in a bucket and lift himself from the ground by the strength of his own muscles. Salvation is in the forgetting of self :

' It is evidence how mortally deep is our self-centredness that even our deliverance from it in respect of many sides of life may become itself an occasion of self-esteem. This is that demon of spiritual pride which most of us are not nearly good enough even to encounter, but which the saints assure us is waiting as it were on the top rung of the ladder of perfection to catch us even there and throw us down. It is not mere self-satisfaction at our own goodness like that of the Pharisee in the parable, though this is often confused with it. It belongs to a far more advanced stage of spiritual progress. It occurs when the self, being by nature self-conscious, which is indeed the condition of all spiritual progress whatever, contemplates its own state of deliverance from self-centredness and finds in that a self-centred satisfaction. It is not merely pride in being good ; it is pride in being delivered from pride ; it is pride in being humble. It turns even self-sacrifice into a form of self-assertion. . . . It is the last effort of the sun of self to keep itself above the horizon. Of course, it is only possible when the deliverance is not complete ; but it is compatible, indeed it is occasioned by, a deliverance which judged from the lower level looks complete. Though so complex in its formula and so insidious in its activity, it is quite simple in its principle. On an altogether lower plane we easily see that wholesome desire is for the objects that will satisfy it, as hunger is desire for food. The satisfaction of the desire brings pleasure ; if desire is now diverted from its appropriate object to the pleasure of attaining or enjoying it, desire is turned into lust. So the proper object of the self's surrender is the Spirit of the Whole which we call God ; but if attention is diverted from God Himself to the self's satisfaction in being surrendered

D—WT

to Him, adoration itself is poisoned. The satisfaction is real, and there is no reason for refraining from attention to it so long as it is in the second place. Man's chief end is to glorify God and (incidentally) to enjoy Him for ever ; but if a man were to say that his end was to enjoy God for ever and (with that aim) to glorify Him, he would be talking pernicious heresy. *The true aim of the soul is not its own salvation ; to make that the chief aim is to ensure its perdition ;* (" Whosoever would save his soul shall lose it."— St. Matthew xvi. 25) *for it is to fix the soul on itself as centre. The true aim of the soul is to glorify God ; in pursuing that aim it will attain to salvation unawares. No one who is convinced of his salvation is as yet even safe, let alone " saved." Salvation is the state of him who has ceased to be interested whether he is saved or not, provided that what takes the place of that supreme self-interest is not a lower form of self-interest, but the glory of God.'* M. pp. 389-391.

' The natural self is capable of disinterested love ; indeed it is probable that every child has for its mother a love which is in part disinterested as soon as it is capable of any true emotion as distinct from animal desire. The vitiation of selfhood by self-centredness is never complete, though it is very persuasive, and there are few children who come to years of so-called discretion in whom self-interest has not contaminated what elements they once had of disinterested love. Yet the capacity for such love is always there in some degree ; it is part of selfhood as God designed and created it. By grace of creation man is made in the image of God, and however much that image may be blurred, it is seldom if ever effaced, and never until the corruption of self-concern has eaten deeply into the very constitution of the self.' M. p. 392.

' The error of the Barthian school of theology—for that it contains error when judged by the canons of either natural reason or Christian revelation I cannot doubt— is, like every other heresy, an exaggeration of truth. To

deny the reality of moral progress, or that moral progress
is an increasing conformity to the Divine, is wanton. To
deny that revelation can, and in the long run must, on pain
of becoming manifest as superstition, vindicate its claim
by satisfying reason and conscience, is fanatical. But that
revelation is altogether other than rational inference from
previous experience is vitally important ; that only by
revelation and by surrender to its spiritual power can man
be " saved," is a profound and irrefragable truth ; that
even when man's salvation is complete there is still the
impassable distinction between Creator and creature,
Redeemer and redeemed, Sanctifier and sanctified, is the
heart of metaphysical and religious sanity. In so far as God
and man are spiritual they are of one kind. But in so far as
God creates, redeems and sanctifies while man is created,
redeemed, and sanctified, they are of two kinds. God is
not creature ; man is not creator. God is not redeemed
sinner ; man is not redeemer from sin. At this point the
Otherness is complete.' M. p. 396.

' *What is quite certain is that the self cannot by any effort
of its own lift itself off its own self as centre and resystem-
atise itself about God as its centre. Such radical conversion
must be the act of God, and that too by some process other
than the gradual self-purification of a self-centred soul
assisted by the ever-present influence of God diffused through
nature including human nature. It cannot be a process only
of enlightenment. Nothing can suffice but a redemptive
act. Something impinging upon the self from without must
deliver it from the freedom which is perfect bondage to the
bondage which is its only perfect freedom.*' M. p. 397.

' The soul or self is free, because nothing outside the
self compels it. And to that very freedom the divine
appeal must be addressed. If God exercised compulsion
by forcing obedience or by remaking the character of a
self against its will, He would have abandoned omnipotence
in the act which should assert it, for the will that was over-

ridden would remain outside His control. The only obedience congruous with the nature of either God or man is an obedience willingly, and therefore freely, offered—a response which is given because the self finds it good to offer it. Our question, therefore, is this : How can the self find it good to submit willingly to removal from its self-centredness and welcome reconstitution about God as its centre ? There is, in fact, one power known to men, and only one, which can effect this, not only for one or another function of the self (as beauty and truth can do), but for the self as a whole in its entirely and its integrity. When a man acts to please one whom he loves, doing or bearing what apart from that love he would not choose to do or bear, his action is wholly determined by the other's pleasure, yet in no action is he so utterly free—that is, so utterly determined by his apparent good. And when love is not yet present, there is one power and only one that can evoke it ; that is the power of love expressed in sacrifice, of love (that is to say), doing and bearing what apart from love would not be willingly done or borne. *The one hope, then, of bringing human selves into right relationship to God is that God should declare His love in an act or acts of sheer self-sacrifice, thereby winning the freely offered love of the finite selves which He has created.'* M. pp. 399, 400.

‘ *All is of God ; the only thing of my very own which I can contribute to my own redemption is the sin from which I need to be redeemed.'* M. p. 401.

‘ We are clay in the hands of the Potter, and our welfare is to know it.' M. p. 403.

ETERNAL LIFE

The Archbishop taught that our moral problem can only be solved as we come to see life as vocation. This raises the question of eternal life, which involves the meaning of history in relation to eternity, and of the moral and religious condition of eternal life. History does not change the Eternal, but if history were different from what it is, the Eternal would be proved to be different from what it is. The Eternal is the ground of the historical, and history has no meaning at all unless eternal life is a reality.

' The Christian hope is not primarily a hope that human society will become the fulfilment of more than Utopian dreams. It is the hope that through the way in which we live and the society wherein we find ourselves, we fit ourselves for fellowship in the great communion of saints, the fellowship of all the servants of God in all the generation, in perpetual communion with Himself.' Aj. p. 22.

Science makes it certain as any statement about the future can be that the world process will come to an end in cold, silence, death, stillness. So that if the process is all that is, it has no meaning, and it is irrelevant to say that this end will come far in the future :

' Astronomers seek to comfort us with the thought that for many millions of years life can continue, and there is plenty of time for our enterprise of progress. That thought brings comfort if the harvest of the world is to be gathered into some eternal store ; but it is sheer lack of imagination to suppose that a vista of a million million years can give more significance than a week or a fortnight to our moral strivings, if at the end it is all to be as though we had never been at all. If that is the end for the race, and all its members pass out of existence, then it is in such a futility that the Eternal finds expression, and nothing can check the attribution of the futility to the Eternal there expressed.' M. p. 449.

' Man's moral and spiritual life is in this world a baffled and thwarted enterprise ; and the scene of our endeavour is slowly becoming uninhabitable, so that even though men labour for a remote posterity yet if this life only is permitted them, it will one day make no difference whether we have striven or not for noble causes and lofty ideals. An earth as cold as the moon will revolve about a dying sun. Duty and love will have lost their meaning. The President of the Immortals, if there be either immortals or president, will have finished his sport with man. And how shall the argument which posited the righteousness of that same Potentate allow us to rest in any such conclusion ? Moreover the worst has not been told. For we have seen that values even of past events may alter, and the value of a whole process depends upon the order of its episodes. A drama which starts in sunshine and ends in gloom has not the same quality in respect of optimism or pessimism as one that starts in gloom and ends in sunshine, though the average tone of the scenes taken separately may be identical ; the drama with a descending scale, so to speak, conveys a sense of even deeper gloom than one that is in the bass register throughout. If at the end there is to be nothing but cold dead cosmos—which might as well be chaos—then, though their presence shines like a jewel in the prevailing gloom, yet it were more creditable to the Determiner of Destiny that virtue and love had never bloomed. That they should appear to be discarded makes the ultimate principle of reality more ruthlessly non-moral than if it had never given birth to them at all. On that hypothesis virtue itself is a blot on the escutcheon of the Maker of the universe and heroism is His deepest shame.' M. p. 452, 453.

In his first considerable book, William Temple was putting the same problem to his readers :

' Our forefathers believed that the world was made in a week, precisely in order that men may dwell upon it ; the heavens were spread out as a canopy over men's heads, and the sun and moon were designed to give light upon the earth. But astronomy came and showed us that this earth of ours, the scene of all our endeavours, is a twirling speck, revolving with quite startling futility about one of the minor stars, always coming back to the same place and always setting out on the ridiculous round again ; and it is growing cold, and where then will be our aspirations and struggles and the cities we have built ? Surely everyone who has looked at the sky on a starry night must have wondered if he is not the merest accident. . . . And, as if this were not enough, Geology followed and revealed incredible vistas in the past history of the earth ; and Biology reduced humanity to a single phase in an endlessly changing life-process. Astronomy made our world a tiny atom in infinite space ; Geology made our whole history a moment in infinite time ; Biology made our boasted faculties an incident in a process whose beginning and end are alike unknown. And so we are left, helpless in a vast machine-like universe, whose indifference to us can only be symbolised by :

> The august, inhospitable, inhuman night
> Glittering magnificently unperturbed.

We find ourselves in a world over whose destiny, in the main, we have no control whatever. It is an ordered world ; and the most important question we can ask is the question —What is the nature and character of the Power or Force that orders it ? This governing principle is not anything that we can do or possess : knowledge of it will not add to our skill in weaving or in carpentering, in medicine or in generalship (Aristotle, *Eth. Nic.* 1097 a 8–13). But without it everything is uncertain, and all resolution becomes infected with ultimate doubt. This knowledge will perhaps not help us to do what we want to do, but it may help us to want to do the right thing.' L. pp. 32, 33.

The chapter on Eternal Life in the Gifford Lectures is of outstanding interest and value. The Archbishop emphasised the fact that the Christian hope of immortality rests on faith in God, and that it is disastrous to invert this order of priority :

' The great aim of all true religion is to transfer the centre
of interest and concern from self to God. Until the doctrine
of God in its main elements is really established, it would
be definitely dangerous to reach a developed doctrine of
immortality. Even when the doctrine of God is established
in its Christian form, the doctrine of immortality can
still, as experience abundantly shows, perpetuate self-
centredness in the spiritual life. If my main concern in
relation to things eternal is to be with the question what is
going to become of *me*, it might be better that I should
have no hope of immortality at all, so that at least as I
look forward into the vista of the ages my Self should not
be a possible object of primary interest.' M. p. 457.

There are three points of importance in the Christian
doctrine. First, it is a doctrine not of immortality but of
resurrection :

' When all is said, there need not be anything religious
in the soul's survival of death or in our conviction that it
survives. That may be a purely natural fact, like waking
from sleep. The Christian doctrine of eternal life is not a
mere proclamation of such survival ; it is a call to life in
fellowship with God, and in Him with our fellows, begun
here and perfected hereafter. Its characteristic expression
is not the immortality of the soul, but the resurrection of the
body. Of course this does not mean the revivification of the
material particles (" flesh and blood cannot inherit the
Kingdom of God "), but the restoration of the whole
personal being in complete continuity with the life lived
here on earth, in a fuller and richer mode of experience
than is possible here and now. We have in this the confident
hope that every grace of character in those whom we have
loved and lost is still theirs in even fuller measure than
during their days on earth.' Aq. p. 7.

Secondly, eternal life is not a natural property of the soul
but is a gift from God. In *Mens Creatrix* he had shown
this as one of the lessons of tragedy :

' If then, I am right in my suggestion that the thought of Immortality is æsthetically admissible in dramas, where the individual characters are throughout regarded as representatives of a spiritual order which they symbolise but do not exhaust, it is legitimate to infer that no man is immortal by right of his individuality, but as he is a member of the whole spiritual world ; or in Pauline language, that it is not as ourselves but as sons of God that we are heirs of eternal life. So Plato represents the Creator as conferring on finite spirits the immortality which He alone possesses by necessity and right.' L. p. 150.

And, thirdly, it is less a doctrine of rewards and punishments than a proclamation of the inherent joy of love and the inevitable misery of selfishness :

' The nature of eternal life—the occupation, so to speak, of the departed—cannot be grasped by us while on earth. " Eye hath not seen, nor ear heard, neither have entered into the heart of man, the things which God hath prepared for them that love Him." But some elements in it are known. Its essential quality is knowledge of God and love to Him and to men—a fading out of self-interest and self-concern in adoration and love. Secondly, it is a life of fellowship—which indeed follows from the first. . . .

' We should try to be conscious of the Communion or Fellowship of Saints, in which our own worship is actually offered. Whenever our worship is genuine, the congregation in which we offer it is not limited to the people gathered in the same building. When we lift up our hearts to the Lord, forthwith it is with angels and archangels and with all the company of heaven that we laud and magnify God's glorious name. In this act of worship we do indeed have communion with our loved ones who have gone before us to the other world.' Aq. p. 5.

Very many people found in William Temple's faith a rock on which they were able to build their own lives. This help and strength were, perhaps, never more manifest

than in the beautiful addresses he gave at funerals. Here
is a quotation from an address in St. Giles's, Oxford, in
memory of Ronald Poulton :

' His Father and ours had other purposes for him. He
has passed by a noble death, still in his splendid beauty
and his glorious youth, to a fuller service of the common
cause than even he could have rendered on earth. And we
know that if ever anyone was at home in the unveiled
Presence of God, it is he. . . . I have never known any one
with so perfectly clear a grasp of all that matters most ;
and he had that because of his perfect loyalty to Christ. . . .
He will not do on earth the work that we had hoped. So
we must do it for him. We shall not do it so well. It is
absurd to speak of following his example. I can no more
acquire his transparency and loveableness than I can acquire
that wonderful swerve which made him the greatest " three-
quarters " that there has ever been. But we can see the
sources of his power and take care never to sin against
them. . . . Simplicity and sympathy ; if we are to do his
work we must never sin against these ; and by these
qualities, more than by any efforts and labours, we shall
do our part to create that fellowship among all men on
which his aspiration was set. . . . Above all we must hold
fast to the unseen hand of our common Master. Some
sorrows make faith difficult, but I do not feel that this is
one of them. A life that is given is not wasted. And all that
has happened in the last ten months has been forcing us to
revise our standards and face life in the light of eternity.
So seen, it is a triumph, not a tragedy, that we commemorate
to-day. . . .

' Christ, who died and is alive for evermore, has overcome the world. By faith in Him—such faith as Ronald
had—we share His triumph. In the assurance of that faith
we banish sadness. Sorrow, indeed, we are bound to feel,
but the sorrow is lit up with hope, and at its very heart
there is a thrilling joy. For though our friend is gone from

our side, we know that he is only gone to a closer union with his Lord, and whenever we lift up our hearts to the Lord, we join with angels and archangels, and all the company of heaven, and there find our friend again. In that faith in that union with the Master, and through the Master with all His followers, we turn back to serve God by serving men, until the time comes for us too to go home, when Ronnie . . . will welcome us, with whatever in the spirit world may be the fulfilment of his infectious laughter, to the nearer presence and the fuller service of the Lord.'

MATTER, LIFE, MIND, SPIRIT

The Archbishop derived from S. Alexander the conception of the universe as existing in a series of grades or *strata*—matter, life, mind, spirit—the lower necessary for the actualising of the higher, but finding the fulness of its being and meaning only when used by the higher as instrument of its self-actualisation. So life needs matter for its expression, but matter reveals what it is only when it is the vehicle of life.

' Similarly, in our experience at least, spirit arises within and as part of an organism which is also material, and expresses its spirituality, not by ignoring matter but by controlling it.' M. p. 477.

' In any organism the distinctive principle of unity is the highest and latest evolved. Man is both a chemical compound, a biological organism, a living mind and a spirit. But the distinctive principle which also gives unity to the whole is spirit. (" I should take as the distinguishing mark of spirit the sense of obligation as distinct from all inclination, however much inclination may itself be swayed by affection." Q. p. 4.) So too in the universe itself, if it is a single system at all, its " highest principle of unity " must be sought in spirit. When we combine this conviction with what has already been said concerning the relation of History to Eternity, we find that we are trying to conceive this relation in a new way. It is not simply the relation of ground and consequence, nor of cause and effect, nor of thought and expression, nor of purpose and instrument, nor of end and means. It finds its closest parallel in a certain element of religious tradition, so that we may best describe this conception of the relation of the eternal to history, of spirit to matter, as sacramental.' M. p. xxx.

'It may safely be said that one ground for the hope of Christianity that it may make good its claim to be the true faith lies in the fact that it is the most avowedly materialist of all the great religions. It affords an expectation that it may be able to control the material, precisely because it does not ignore it or deny it, but roundly asserts alike the reality of matter and its subordination. Its own most central saying is : " The Word was made flesh," where the last term was, no doubt, chosen because of its specially materialistic associations. By the very nature of its central doctrine Christianity is committed to a belief in the ultimate significance of the historical process, and in the reality of matter and its place in the divine scheme.' M. p. 478.

'It may be true of any—or every—particular man that in fact he behaves for the most part exactly as he would if he had no spiritual capacity. But even when this is true of his acts, it is not true of his action in doing them. When a being capable of spiritual discrimination blindly obeys an appetite, this is not, as moral conduct, identical with obedience to the same appetite on the part of an animal which has no spiritual discrimination. In the animal it is natural, even when to human taste it is distressing ; in the man it is evidence of defect when it is not proof of depravity. In that distinction is implicit the naturally controlling efficacy of spirit wherever it is present at all.' M. p. 479.

EVIL, SIN, AND FORGIVENESS

For such a philosophy of theism the problem of evil is peculiarly obstinate and acute :

' The problem of evil becomes all the greater in proportion as you insist on the character of the ultimate Being. It is only those people who have a vivid conception and conviction of the holiness of God who are sharply brought up against the problem of evil. You find it governing the Hebrew literature as it does no other ancient literature, because the Hebrews felt the contradiction between their experience and the Holy God to whom in their worship they had drawn near. You find it pretty strong in Plato, because he has a great conviction that only Good can explain things. It is hardly present in Aristotle, who has not that great conviction and whose doctrine of the ultimate source of being is arrived at by a line of physical argument—the necessity of a being who can set things in motion without itself being set in motion by anything else. It is in proportion as men believe in the character of the infinite Spirit that they are brought up against evil in the finite world.' P. pp. 53, 54.

' To all who think the world must at times appear overwhelming in the perplexity it causes ; and some will always feel bound to say that they see no track through the maze. Such agnosticism—reverent and tentative, not blatant and aggressive—is the cost some men must pay if mankind is to find truth at last. We who are Christians remember that the Godhead never shone forth in Christ so effulgently as in the moment when He felt Himself forsaken of God ; and we shall not think ill of those who, in the search for truth, fill up what remains of the sufferings of Christ. But we still believe—though often with doubt and trembling—that the secret of the universe is made known to us in Christ. As we use our belief the problem seems to dissolve ; the path of duty becomes clearer, and the darkness which surrounds our minds is no longer a thick blackness, but a mist through which we grope our way. For in Christ we see the perfect union of physical and spiritual, and in His death we see God bearing the evil of the world. But if so—?

' " The very God " think, Abib. . . . ' Af. pp. xxxi, xxxii.

The Archbishop's steady reaction to the problem of evil was to say that the reasonable attitude is not, ' This is good, therefore it must be real ! ' or ' This is evil, therefore it must be explained ! ' but that which asks concerning every situation which arises, how good may be won out of it, and how even what is evil in it may be made subservient to good.

' Man is so great in and through the struggle, and good so glorious that we would not have the evil simply abolished ; for that would be to abolish the struggle, and with it much of the greatness and the glory. The world revealed in tragedy is a noble world, and better than any we can conceive—yet it is terrible and pitiful and sad beyond belief. We would not alter it ; yet we cannot be content with it. This is the Philosophy of Tragedy ; and if it is not the last word of human philosophy, at least we know that no philosophy can by any possibility be true which does not contain it, or which diminishes in any degree whatsoever the depths of its exalted sad solemnity.' L. p. 152.

In general he dares to say that although evil is really evil, in many respects the world, with the evil in it, is better than it could be but for the evil. For instance :

' Error, then, may be regarded as the symptom of the adventurous character of the intellectual life ; if it were impossible, that character would be gone ; if it were never actual, that character would be unperceived and therefore valueless. The justification of each particular error must be sought in the circumstances of its origin and the joy of its removal. But in general terms we may say that part of the real excellence of the life of reason depends, not accidentally but essentially, upon the existence of error.' L. p. 278.

' I can only assert my own judgment that there are cases of suffering which, by drawing out our real sympathy (I mean, of course, what Mr. McDougall calls " Sympathy in the fullest sense of the word " (*Social Psychology*, p. 173), such as is effective in overcoming the suffering, are justified ; the existence of the suffering and the sympathy together is better than the absence of both. The sympathy takes the pain into itself and makes it an element in its own good. It is true that the average tolerably selfish man can only be roused to real sympathy by the sight of real pain (Cf. Browning, *Ferishtah's Fancies : Mihrab Shah*) ; but that is not the point I wish to emphasise, for it seems that so far the dependence of the sympathy on the suffering is accidental. But there is a peculiar quality about sympathy of this kind which *consists* in the nature of its object, and it is a quality of supreme excellence. Pain, coupled with fortitude in its endurance, especially when this is inspired by love, and meeting the full sympathy which at first lightens it and at last destroys it by removal of its grounds, is sometimes the condition of what is best in human life.' L. p. 278.

' For all the anguish of the world there are three consolations. The Epicurean says, " It is but for a time ; ere long we shall fall asleep in the unending slumber " ; which is comfort of a sort. The Stoic says, " Rise above it all ; to the wise these things are nugatory " : which is no comfort at all if we are not wise. Christianity says, " Christ also suffered " ; and that, with the Christian interpretation of " Christ," is real consolation, a human answer to our humanity.' L. pp. 279, 280.

' To justify the actual sufferings of men we must seek them out and extend our sympathy, spending ourselves in the removal of pain and sorrow which are elements in the good of the world precisely, but only, so far as they are overcome. " There is no general answer to the problem of evil, but a particular answer whenever it is embraced as suffering and confessed as sin " (A. C. Turner in *Concerning Prayer*, p. 382). The theoretical and the practical are not two functions, but one, and it is not sensible to give one a priority over the other. Always our aim is to systematise or harmonise experience ; sometimes the mind does this by " thinking," sometimes by " acting " ; to leave out any of the mind's functions will make it incapable of the full apprehension of Reality. The evil we are considering is not a concept, but is the actual pains and sorrows of men. To make a harmony of these, within the beneficent Purpose of God as so far understood, involves not the concept of sympathy but actual sympathising effort. In the degree in which we are capable of love we have the right to say to any who in this world are in tribulation, " I have overcome the world." ' L. p. 281.

If, in practice, there is no way of conquering evil, then, theoretically, theism is refuted. That is the problem of evil, of course, and if the statement of it in *Mens Creatrix* seems somewhat cool and academic, it must be remembered that that book was an Essay in Philosophy. That the Archbishop *felt* the problem intensely appears often in his writings. Of this the following passage is an illustration :

' The only religious problem that I have ever come across in any one that I have met, constituting a real hindrance to religious conviction, is the problem of evil, a problem vividly and tersely stated once in a discussion by a working man who described the appalling story of his wife's sufferings, and ended by saying, " If Jesus were God, that would not happen." In one way or another, the great problem of the religious life arises precisely from the fact that our consciences claim the right, and exercise the right, of criticising God as we know Him. It becomes, therefore, more and more clear that conscience itself is not simply the channel through which belief about God issues into conduct ; it is something independent of our religious life.' Aa. p. 57.

Dr. Temple's treatment of the more serious aspect of the problem of evil, that of sin, is on similar lines :

' What is the essence of sin ? All the actions which make up its particular manifestations are the satisfaction of impulses which have a true place in the economy of life and can be morally exercised. But as all morality consists in the recognition of the claims of other spirits whether Divine or human, so does all sin consist in the ignoring or repudiation of those claims. . . . Indifference, hostility, and fellowship are the only primary relations that are possible between one man and another ; and the former two, except as regulated by the last, are immoral. The essence of sin is self-will. By pride Satan fell in the myth, and the myth is right. Of the forms of self-will, complete indifference to other people is the worst. Hatred at least recognises the other person as being of importance, and in essence, as well as by our psychological tendencies, is nearer to the moral relation with its culmination in love than is indifference.' L. p. 285.

He has a word for those, inside the Church as well as outside it, who deprecate ' this sin obsession ' :

' If anyone feels that the language which the Church asks him to use is exaggerated—" We do earnestly repent and are heartily sorry for these our misdoings ; the remembrance of them is grievous unto us ; the burden of them is intolerable "—then let him think of slums, and sweating and prostitution, and war, and ask if the remembrance of these is not grievous, and if the burden of them ought not to be intolerable. Let him remember that these horrible things are there, not because some men are outrageously wicked, but because millions of men are as good as we are, and no better.' B . p.44.

And he states simply and clearly, and with a poignant understanding, the essential irrationality of sin :

' We know it is morally wrong, and we know it is self-destructive, yet rather than pluck out our right eye, rather even than close it, we fling our whole body into hell. It is no use trying to find reasons for doing this ; reason is all on the other side, as we know quite well when we act. We do not even think the present good greater than the more remote. We do not think at all. We just say, " Here goes ! " ' Af. p. 42.

The winning of the knowledge of good and evil is called the Fall of Man because, in the process, mere instinctive reactions to environment become sins against the light, and done against the light, they involve a new degree of self-assertion. It was not utterly necessary that man should become self-centred and self-assertive in this false and sinful way :

' It was not utterly necessary that this should be so ; and therefore it is not true to say that God made man selfish, or predestined him to sin. But that it should be so was " too probable not to happen " ; and it is true to say that God so made the world that man was likely to sin, and the dawn of moral consciousness was more likely to be a " fall " than an ascent. Human sin was not a necessary episode in the divine plan ; but was always so closely implicated in the divine plan that it must be held to fall within the divine purpose.' M. p. 366.

Because we are members one of another, the self-centred-ness of each makes others more self-centred. So the force of selfishness accumulates to the destruction of the world :

' This may, perhaps, be called an evolutionary account of the origin of moral evil. But it must be sharply distinguished from any theory of moral evil which accounts for it by reference to a survival of animal impulses into the rational stage of development. The centre of trouble is not the turbulent appetites, though they are troublesome enough, and the human faculty for imagination increases their turbulence. But the centre of trouble is the personality as a whole, which is self-centred and can only be wholesome and healthy if it is God-centred. This whole personality in action is the will ; and it is the will which is perverted. Our primary need is not to control our passions by our purpose, but to direct our purpose itself to the right end. It is the form taken by our knowledge of good and evil that perverts our nature. We know good and evil, but know them amiss. We take them into our lives, but we mistake them. The corruption is at the centre of rational and purposive life.' M. p. 367.

' The most vital point is that reason itself as it exists in us is vitiated. We wrongly estimate the ends of life, and give preference to those which should be subordinate, because they have a stronger appeal to our actual, empirical selves. That is why the very virtues of one generation lead to the miseries of the next ; for they are contaminated with the evil principle, and it is truly said that " our right-eousnesses are filthy rags." *We totally misconceive alike the philosophic and the practical problem of evil if we picture it as the winning of control over lawless and therefore evil passions by a righteous but insufficiently powerful reason or spirit. It is the spirit which is evil ; it is aspiration itself which is corrupt.*' M. p. 368.

But even this demonic Pride and self-willed irrationality find a meaning in the Love of God :

' But if sin is essentially Self-will in one or another of these forms, why is there Self-will ? And I answer quite confidently : because Love is never so completely itself as when it enters on complete self-surrender to conquer the indifferent or the hostile and succeeds. This is not due to any accident. Love is not only a motive to self-surrender, but rather, as Nettleship said, " Love is the consciousness of survival in the act of self-surrender." The fact that there is more joy over one sinner that repenteth than over ninety and nine just persons who need no repentance is based upon the further fact that love perfects itself by the conquest of hostility by self-surrender. . . . So far forth as the self-surrender of love is made absolute, love becomes completely itself and supremely excellent. . . . When the self-surrender is complete, the manifestation of the eternal glory and excellency of God is complete also. But the self-surrender cannot be complete if there is not the utmost opposition that can be quelled. Love whose return is achieved by struggle is better than spontaneous affection, not accidentally but essentially ; for the specific ardour of the struggle enters into the fibre of the love itself. In fact a sinful world redeemed by the agony of Love's complete self-sacrifice is a better world, by the only standards of excellence we have, than a world that had never sinned. " O felix culpa, quae talem et tantum meruit habere redemptorem ! " . . . And, of course, it is only so far as self-will is conquered by love that it is justified as an element in the world's history. But when conquered it is justified. It may become good for me that I have sinned, that I may love God as my Redeemer ; (Cf. the well-known hymn :

'There's a song for little children'
   Above the bright blue sky,
A song that will not weary
   Though sung continually,
A song which even angels
   Can never never sing ;
They know not Christ as Saviour,
   But worship Him as King.)

' it may prove good for Him that I have sinned, that He may have the joy of my redemption. We postponed the justification of the suffering that is bravely borne because it is inspired by love ; but we have found it here.' L. pp. 286, 287.

'If we would realise what our sin means to God, we see it in the Cross. If we would know how He regards us as we wound Him, we see it in Christ during the Passion. No man can go on for ever wounding one who bears the blow like that ; no man is insensitive to love if once he realises that he is loved. We may wantonly persist even in the injury of love, but not for ever. Love, if understood, always prevails at last ; and it does so by making itself known ; and it makes itself known by sacrifice. The sacrifice of the love of God is the means by which sin is conquered ; it is God's sacrifice of Himself, and therefore may reach and conquer all at last. And in conquering the sin, it justifies it ; for the love thereby developed and won back is richer and deeper than is possible without the struggle (Cf. Luke vii. 47 ; xv. 3–10). The Principle of Reason which governs the world is the eternal victory of Love over selfishness at the cost of sacrifice. This is not proved, of course, but it is credible ; it makes sense, and nothing else makes sense, of sin.' Ar. pp. 221, 222.

'If we are compelled not only to say but to feel that in the Passion of Christ we see a picture of God, and of the way in which God regards our moral state, immediately the whole of our own feeling about that moral state is absolutely changed from the foundation. I say, if we feel it ; for what is it that we are feeling? We are feeling that the great Power which rules the world is submitting to suffer at our hands, in a way which can only be represented by the agony of Christ, and regards us as we inflict that agony in the way in which Christ regarded the people who sent Him to the Cross. When He is reviled He reviles not again, when He suffers He threatens not : "Father, forgive them ; for they know not what they do." If we really feel that, it becomes intolerable. It is like finding that, without knowing what one did, one had struck one's mother in the face. That is why the religious life can make all the difference to morality, because to the religious man all his faults, which he will now call his sins, are no longer merely a breach of law ; they are the betrayal of a friend. They were wrong before ; and he knew it, but he did not mind. But the religious man must mind.' Aa. pp. 63, 64.

' Until Christ came, every image of God was an idol ; until Christ died, every conception of the Divine Love was soft and sentimental, unless it were balanced, as we see it balanced in the Prophets, by an element of sternness which may be logically incompatible with the other, but is morally necessary. Forgiveness of sins is demoralising, unless it is offered at overwhelming cost to the pardoner. If God merely says, " Never mind," that is an insult to the better kind of man and an encouragement to the worse kind. But when God has set forth the tremendous cost at which alone He can forgive, everything is changed. There is nothing so humbling as that one's friend should say— " You have betrayed me, and no words can express the pain it caused ; but it shall not disturb our friendship." There is nothing in that demoralising, nor anything that can encourage the basest.' As. pp. 72, 73.

' Whether forgiveness is good for a wrong-doer or not entirely depends on how much it costs the person who forgives. As a result of indifference it does harm ; as a result of love for the sinner conquering hate of the sin it does good.' Aa. p. 86.

' What it costs God to forgive man is shown in the Cross ; and if a man is feeling that what he has done involves agony to One who none the less forgives him, he is not going to take offence at being forgiven ; and if he feels that what he does cost agony to One who none the less forgives him, he is not going to say, " It does not matter ; I can do it again." . . . When we come to understand it, forgiveness is seen to be the greatest glory of God. Then, apparently, the more we sin the better ? . . . How can we any longer go on sinning as if it were a matter of perfect indifference ? The state of mind in which the desire to glorify God arises is incompatible with the committing of wrong actions.   Further, forgiveness of the kind that Christianity promises is the strongest of all motives to change of character. . . .   But if anyone should say that what morality demands is that a man should face the consequences of his acts and bear them, and that what will keep a man from wrong-doing is simply a fear of those consequences, so that the promise of forgiveness by weakening that fear destroys morality, I should answer that the kind of justice which he is upholding is in itself quite valueless, and as a motive it is quite or almost ineffective. I wonder how many people there are whose conduct is genuinely affected by the thought of Hell ; they must be extremely few.   But the number of people whose conduct is affected by the belief that their wrong-doing means to God what is set before us in the Cross are very many. It is a stronger motive and it is a better motive, for it is an appeal not to a man's selfishness, but to his generosity. In it is a motive which, in checking wrong-doing, also develops the tendency to good, which fear of punishment can never do.   So what I would claim for the religion of the Christian is that as it alone does justice to every side of human nature, so it alone constantly appeals to what is highest in human nature.   Should we prefer people if they responded mainly to the fear of punishment or mainly to some bare conception of abstract duty?   Or do we prefer men who respond to the appeal of sympathy, of love, and of devotion ?   If the latter, then remembering that the appeal to any motive always strengthens that motive, we shall say that this, and this alone, is the ground upon which character can be developed, and on which alone it is desirable that it should be developed.'   Aa. pp. 126-129.

' Thus all history appears as the method of the Divine Love.   That love requires beings whom it may love, and requires their varying forms of evil for the perfecting of love.   Inasmuch as it is love, it enters by sympathy into all

pain and sorrow, and spends itself in the redemptive agony.
Eternally it operates. From the infinite past to the infinite
future it continues its course of irresistible victory; at every
stage there is advance ; every epoch has its own determinate
goal to reach, and in reaching it finds that new problems
arise. The endless growth of the world provides for ever
new material on which love may exercise itself, and we
witness the continually wider application of a principle to
whose application no limit is set either by the principle
itself or by the nature of the subject matter. Yet the victory
is that not of force but of tenderness, and the Word of God
which goes forth conquering and to conquer must be first
symbolised by the figure of a Lamb as it had been slain.'
L. p. 290.

THE INCARNATION

Just as the Archbishop held that a philosophical case
can be made for theism, but that it must be confirmed by,
and in its turn must confirm, ordinary religious experience,
so he held that the religious interpretation of the universe,
and the behaviour appropriate to such an interpretation,
can only be confidently maintained and consistently
carried out on the basis of the Incarnation.

'If the Gospel is a myth, agnosticism is at least as
scientific as faith ; but if Jesus lived and died and rose
again, then God must be His Father.' L. p. 292.

'What we watch in the formative period of Christian
theology is indeed a perpetual expansion of the conception
of God under the influence of the revelation in Christ ;
but, for the most part, it seems fair to say that neither
then, nor at any time since then, have men, so to speak,
integrated their Christology with their theology, or given
full value, theologically, to the words, " He that hath seen
Me hath seen the Father." ' Ab. p. 224.

'Then comes the marvel of the Gospel, wistfully perceived by Prophets and Psalmists as from afar, but never by them apprehended as the crowning glory of the all-glorious ; this God of Power, so great that before Him the inhabitants of the earth are grasshoppers, who taketh up the isles as a very little thing—this God is Love ; not merely kindly with the condescension of an emperor to a beggar child, but love such as is manifest in Jesus Christ, so that the way in which He expresses Divine authority is by performing the act of menial service.

' And, therefore, though He has no need of us for the fullness of His being, He has need of us for the satisfaction of His love. Though we can add nothing to Him, nor take anything away, yet He entrusts Himself and His cause to us, that He may have the joy of receiving, and we the blessedness of giving, willing service. His love is very tender, but it is bracing, not indulgent. He is Love, and knows love to be the best thing that there is ; therefore, for love's sake, He will be very stern with us when we turn away from that best That we should become content with our selfishness would be the worst thing that could happen to us, and He relentlessly besets the way of selfishness with calamity that men may not sink back into the slough from which His love is ever calling them.' Ag. pp. 537, 538.

' The life of Christ is a momentary manifestation of eternal truth, and it is good for us as a devotional exercise sometimes to read the Gospels, turning all the past tenses into the present, and to remember that what we read there is the expression, quite strictly . . . under all conditions of the time and place in which the expression occurred, of what is always true. And the culmination of this utterance is the Passion. The ultimate truth about God and His relation to finite spirits is this, that " when He is reviled He reviles not again, and when He suffers, He threatens not." Now that is the only possible mode of omnipotence in a world that contains free finite spirits. Once God had been pleased to create beings with hearts and souls capable of choosing for themselves—and therefore morally certain to choose for themselves in the special sense of choosing what they like for themselves—there was only one way by which He could be omnipotent ; it must be by revelation of His love in such a form as to win answering love. There can be no other. He could have controlled external events, of course ; He could have controlled our conduct, by sheer exercise of power ; but then there would have been something that finally and for ever escaped His sovereignty —the heart and will of man, the highest thing He had made, the thing for which perhaps much of the rest was made. If that was to be won, it must be won in such a way that its allegiance was no contradiction of its freedom. Now it is a perfectly common experience that when we do things to please other people, our action is determined by what is their pleasure, and yet our freedom is never so complete. There is no act in which a man is so entirely self-determining as when he deliberately acts for the sake of another's pleasure or another's welfare. He does not in the least degree feel that he has been hypnotised or his will over-ridden, or that he is a mere passive instrument, reduced to a puppet by the other's will. On the contrary, he is then most of all himself ; we know it perfectly well. There is all the difference in the world between acting in this way from love and acting under a kind of coercion that some powerful personality has put upon us without carrying our consent with him. If God is to become the determinant of our conduct in such a way as not to paralyse the will and heart that He has made, it must be by winning our love ; and there is only one way, broadly speaking, in which our love is drawn out to those to whom it does not spontaneously go.' P. pp. 69–71.

' The goal is the Kingdom of God, the sovereignty of Love—such love as God had shown upon the Cross. But the focus of history is that disclosure itself, so that history will still be full of meaning even though the wilfulness of men prevents us from going forward under the attraction of that love into a fuller and fuller fellowship between man and God and man with man. It will still be judged by its relationship to the Cross, for purpose, for policy, for choice, and for ambition, and find its standard of reference there.

' How does it look in the light of that ?—with the knowledge that what is there set forth is the eternal God into fellowship with whom it is our destiny, unless we frustrate it, to enter, so that elsewhere if not here the perfect fellowship of love shall be built up, through the power and the redeeming love of God in Christ and the power of the Holy Spirit quickened in the hearts of men in answer to it ? . . . It was, in fact, for his redemption that Christ did come, and it remains a fact that only in the power that is discoverable in the Cross can man turn history into the thing that God designed it to be and in which he may find his own satisfaction.' Aj. pp. 19–21.

' So we come to the central declaration, more central for Christian faith than even *The Word became Flesh ;* for that depends for its inexhaustible wealth of meaning on the actual mode of the Incarnate Life. But here is the whole great truth. *God so loved the world that He gave His only begotten Son, that everyone that believeth on Him may not perish but have eternal Life.* That is the heart of the Gospel. Not " God is Love "—a precious truth but affirming no divine act for our redemption. *God so loved that He gave ;* of course the words indicate the cost to the Father's heart. *He gave ;* it was an act, not only a continuing mood of generosity ; it was an act at a particular time and place. " Blessed be the Lord God of Israel "—it is not a universally diffused divine essence of which we speak, but the Living God—" for He *hath visited and redeemed* His people."

' No object is sufficient for the love of God short of *the world* itself. Christianity is not one more religion of individual salvation, differing from its fellows only in offering a different road to that goal. It is the one and only religion of world-redemption. Of course, it includes a way of individual salvation as the words before and after this great saying show. But its scope is wider than that—as wide as the love of God. It is a *sin of the world* that Christ takes away (i. 29).' Au. vol. 1, p. 48.

' Only a portion of any material substance could be manifested in a particular place or at a particular time. But that is not true of quality, which is the category appropriate to spirit. People sometimes say : " How much of God was revealed in Christ ? If you believe as a Christian that God was revealed in Christ, how much of Him was revealed ? " Well, all of Him that is relevant : His love, and His holiness, which is part of His love, is all there. If the love that was in Christ was a perfect love for all men, there is nothing that can make it any greater, for it is already an infinite. You have reached a logical limit beyond which it is self-contradictory that you should ask to go ; there cannot be more love than absolute self-giving to all.' P. p. 48.

' In any life you do have the necessary, the unique, the irreplaceable expression of the spirit that dominates that life ; and further, . . . in the degree in which that spirit is strong and pure it gives unity to the life, setting all its phases and all its actions in the right proportion ; and above all this . . . the exactness and the fullness of the expression entirely depends upon the particularity of the conduct. If you have a man who is full of religion and good-will towards mankind, pursuing the even tenor of his way in a moderately comfortable existence in a small villa in the suburbs of a town, distributing his charity with genial good-nature and so forth, but otherwise living like anybody else, you get in such a form of life comparatively little opportunity of expression for the spirit which is the universal truth behind it, just because it is so like the lives of other people ; just because it is so general, it fails to express the universal, not because there is a conflict between the general and the universal, but because there is conflict between expression and generality. Every artist knows that a universal only finds expression in what is perfectly individual. Indeed, individuality is the perfect synthesis between universal and particular, and if either fails the individuality is lessened. The more detailed you make the expression, the better expression it will be, provided the spirit expressed is always constant. If it is, then you will still have a unity of all the diverse detailed pieces of conduct. Consequently we shall not be surprised to find in that Life, for which the claim is made that it expresses the universal Spirit, that it belongs to a particular time and a particular place, that it was lived under the conditions of a comparatively narrow circle of people, sharply marked off from all others, that it fully accepts these limitations and expresses itself in and through them. On the contrary, we shall rejoice in all that. It is only through such particularity that our Lord can give any detailed expression, which means any real expression, of the universality of His love. Love above all things requires such expression ; because love must show itself in service to this one and that one under the conditions of their existence. It cannot be shown merely on the broad scale and in general terms. It must be individual. Therefore, in the close relationship between our Lord's historical ministry and the conditions of His time the Christian will find no difficulty or perplexity at all ; for what is important to him is not that the Lord did this particular thing or uttered this particular precept, but that in all of these you find one single spirit pervading the whole life, and that a spirit of such kind that it can find its operation everywhere in all times and in all places, and through all persons of all races.

' For there is one other requirement which a spiritual philosophy will make of any universal principle if it is to

be accepted as the explanation of the world. What is it ?
It is that the spirit itself must be such as can operate plainly
in all places. Now there are two great goals set before us
by St. John in his First Epistle which I have been taking
as a sort of guiding star of our thought in these lectures,
which you can always pursue with absolute perfection,
though one of them with more thoroughness of success
than the other, so that your devotion to them can always
be complete and active. One is truth and one is love. You
can always not only desire the truth, as you can always
desire beauty, but you can always be actively promoting it,
as you cannot always be creating beauty ; you can always
be so directing your mind that you are furthering the cause
of truth in the world. Truth to all fact, and truth in all
thought. But you may not always be able to attain to the
truth you seek. Love is always supreme over the world
in this sense at least—there is no conceivable situation in
which it is not possible to show absolute perfection of love.
I do not think there is any other quality of which that can
be said. At least it is true of love; and the infinite Spirit
for whom it is claimed that he is the source of all being
and the explanation of the world must be at least this,
whatever else besides—perfect and absolute love. Nothing
else corresponds with this very obvious fact of universal
experience. In one sense it is so obvious that one is almost
ashamed to labour the point ; but it is also overwhelmingly
important that wherever you are you can always practise
and show love. Does it not tell you a good deal about this
universe in which we live, that love is one of the things,
possibly the only thing, that can never be excluded by
circumstance ? ' P. pp. 58–61.

Creation and Redemption. The University Sermon at
Cambridge, Septuagesima, 1925.

' " God said, Let there be light ; and there was light."
(Gen. i. 3).

' " Jesus cried with a loud voice . . . My God, My

God, why hast Thou forsaken Me ? " (St. Matt. xv. 34).

' Those two sayings measure the distance in effort and cost between creation and redemption. The one is so easy ; the utterance of the command effects its fulfilment. The other is so infinitely hard that it can only be represented by the attribution of a sense of failure to the Incarnate Word of God. The one consorts naturally with the popular notion of Omnipotence ; the other belongs to a thought of God which conceives Him as Almighty only by His own self-sacrifice. The thought of God as Creator of the Universe has always suggested such a conception of Him as makes very difficult any full acceptance of the Passion. The thought of the evil in the world and of God as Redeemer suggests a conception of Him which easily leads men to deny His Omnipotence altogether. But here, as so often, the whole Christian belief consists in a balance of two conceptions apparently incompatible, not by the paring away of each until the incompatibility vanishes through the disappearance of all that is significant in both conceptions, but by the setting of each in its own place in a scheme which has room for both.

' The thought of our time has more difficulty with the Omnipotence than with the Passion of God, and is often ready to deny the doctrine of Creation in the interest of that of Redemption. Theories which present to us a purely immanent Deity, who by His efforts and sacrifices carries forward the process of history, are of this type. . . . But a few generations back the tendency was all in the other direction, as, no doubt, it will one day be again. On the whole the Victorian Age accepted Creation more readily, and stumbled at Redemption. In the eighteenth century the function of Deity was commonly reduced to Creation only, and, according to the prevalent Deism of that period, God having made the world and launched it on its way, thenceforth took no more action in reference to it.

' There are very few propositions seriously advanced by

thoughtful men which can with reasonable fairness be called false. In themselves they are nearly always true ; but by a too summary logic men often suppose that the truth of some one proposition involves the falsity of another, when in fact they can quite harmoniously stand side by side. The change we have noted from the eighteenth to the twentieth century is the theological form of the transference of philosophic attention from Fact to Value. God as supreme over the world of mere existence is Creator ; God as supreme over Good and Evil is Redeemer. An age dominated by Physics will give first place to the former ; an age dominated by History, Politics, and Psychology will give first place to the latter. But both are there to be taken into account ; and it is part of the glory of the Christian doctrine that it does take account of them. . . .

' Christians must surely rejoice at the perpetually greater place given to value, as compared with mere existence, in recent philosophy. There is a long step in the matter of emphasis from Bradley's *Appearance and Reality* to Bosanquet's Gifford Lectures on *Individuality and Value*. The use in those lectures of the pregnant phrase of Keats describing the world as a vale of soul making, represents a big transition towards the religious and Christian standpoint. Others have carried the movement still further, with the result that the general character of philosophic thought to-day is spiritual as it has hardly been (except in Spinoza) since the Middle Ages. But we must not let this most welcome tendency diminish its own fruitfulness by onesided and unbalanced neglect of what had been strong in the older way of thinking. The idea of God which consorts with a philosophy of existence is that of the Creator who causes things to be ; the idea of God which consorts with a philosophy of value is an immanent and informing Spirit. But reality is fact and value in one, and our thought of God must be true to both aspects.

' Provided, however, that belief in the Creator be not

lost, it is faith in the Redeemer which lifts religion to the Christian level ; and so we return to the thought from which we started. No one who has thought of God as Creator has conceived Him as putting forth effort to create. The Word is self-accomplishing. " Let there be Light ; and there was Light." Myriads of worlds following their appointed course through the vastness of space exist because He would have it so. But that self-willed souls should be won to love Him, and thus make love and not self the centre of their being—that costs what is represented by Gethsemane and the Cross. The world as a vale of soul making is full of darkness and tragedy, into which God Himself must enter.

' There can be no stronger assertion than this of the superiority of spirit over matter. The physical universe is to the Almighty " a very little thing " ; What else is meant by calling Him Almighty ? But not every task is even to Him a little thing. The fashioning of a child's soul is a task to call from Incarnate God the Bloody Sweat and the Cry of Desolation. So much greater and more precious is a moral being than all the majesty of the starry heavens. And when we remember who it is who was Incarnate, the mingled reverence and fear of our worship becomes a loved-filled awe in presence of God, " who for us men and for our salvation came down from heaven . . . and was made man."

' The glory of God is declared by the heavens, and by the firmament which is His handiwork. But we, who know a glory higher still, might address to God words suggested by those of the Prophet to the Servant of the Lord : it is too light a thing that Thou shouldest call worlds into being out of nothingness. Thou shalt turn pride into humility and call out love from the selfish heart.' R.

' The Gospel is precisely the proclamation of the good news that God exists and is eternally what we see in Jesus Christ. . . . It is worth while to point to the importance

E—WT

of the fact that the revelation is given in a Person and not
in a set of propositions—not even in a set of propositions
about that Person. It is to Christ, not to the Creed, that
the world is to look for its salvation. The Creed is important because it points to the one hope of Redemption ; but
its importance is secondary, for it is not itself the source of
saving power. Remembrance of this will save us from the
central mediæval blunder of imposing the rule of theology
on science or art, or *enforcing* a submission of conduct to
religion. The unity we seek must come from the all-
pervasiveness of the influence and spirit of a Person. The
message of the Gospel to individuals, to groups, to classes,
to nations, to races, is " Let this mind be in you which
was also in Christ Jesus," and the same message is given
to economists, to scientists, to artists, to poets, to novelists,
to journalists. Moreover, it declares that this is possible
just because Jesus Christ is not only a historic figure like
Socrates or Cæsar but is the manifestation of that universal
and eternal Spirit in whom we live and move and have
our being, and who is Himself the source of our existence
and sustainer of our life." Z. pp. 26, 27.

What all this means is that in the Incarnation as it actually
happened is the clue to the meaning of nature and history :

' What we see in Him is what we should see in the history
of the universe if we could apprehend that history in its
completeness. And even then it is to be remembered that
we have not the World-History without the Incarnation
as one expression of the Divine Will and the Life of the
Incarnate as another ; for that Life is a part of History,
though it reveals the principle of the whole, and it is
through its occurrence in the midst of History that History
is fashioned into an exposition of the principle there
revealed. We have here a series which is part of another
series and yet is perfectly representative of it. (Cf. the
Supplementary Essay in Royce's *The World and the Individual*.) But here the series which is contained (the Life,

Death, Resurrection of Christ) only becomes representative of the series which contains it (the entire history of the world) in virtue of the influence which by occurring within the latter it is able to exercise upon it. Therefore, though Transcendence and Immanence are fused into one, the Transcendent aspect is always dominant.' L. p. 318.

It was not primarily His teaching but Himself which is the final revelation of God :

' It was altogether contrary to His whole method of teaching that He should say in so many words, This prophecy or that was true in one respect, but inadequate in another ; or, to be more precise, that He should say quite plainly that His Kingdom was to rest solely upon the power of love. To say such things in the form of direct instructions would frustrate the very object in view ; it would set up a theory of the Kingdom before the Kingdom itself was there. But He would live among men and die before men, manifesting Himself His Resurrection, so that those who had been witnesses of these things would be banded together in an actual Kingdom long before they had any theory about the nature of that Kingdom or its basis. In this way their whole natures, their aims and purposes no less than their intellectual ideas, would be won for His service, and this could be accomplished in no other way." L. p. 336.

' This, I submit, is the impression left on the open-minded reader of the Gospels. They tell the story of a human life ; but humanity is not the last word about it. He who so lived is not self-occupied or concerned with doctrines of His own Person. But He spontaneously and with conscious appropriateness does what only God can do. At times, as spiritual occasion arises, the implications of this come vividly before His mind. He is not self-analytical but He is self-revealing : and the self that He reveals is more than human, more than superhuman ; it is specifically divine.' O. p. 123.

Limitations of space make it impossible to give anything like an adequate selection from what William Temple wrote on the acts and words of Jesus. A few quotations will illustrate his knowledge, his insight and his exegetical power :

' Not in the News.

' No one knew it was happening. That is as important as almost any other fact about it. Herod did not know ; he found out a little later and " re-acted," as we say now-a-days, with totalitarian thoroughness. The High Priest did not know ; he was maintaining his precarious balance between a Government which might disestablish him and a crowd of devotees who were fanatically anti-Erastian. The innkeeper did not know ; he was doing a roaring trade with all the folk who had come to their birth-place to fill in the census-return. No one knew.

' Well, not quite " no-one." Some shepherds had an inkling about it, it seems they had been oddly affected by the silence and loneliness of their night watch, and some obscure process of psychological compensation, as some people are liable to say now-a-days, projected against the irresponsive heavens a vision of celestial companions. And Joseph was not quite without understanding of the event. And Mary—but we will not let the clumsy fingers of modern speculation play upon the exquisite mystery of her surrender, her readiness to receive what God should give, her wondering exaltation of her lowliness which the Lord had regarded. Yet even she, though rapt in adoring gratitude, did not know what it was that was happening. In that sense of the words, no one knew. . . .

' I don't know what Augustus was doing that night ; if it had any public reference, no doubt he and everyone about him thought it very important. If an angel had come to him instead of to the shepherds and had said, " Leave all this alone ; it does not matter ; nothing matters tonight except the fact that a poor woman has had a baby in a stable "—Augustus and his courtiers would have thought a lunatic was playing a practical joke on them ; or else that, having presumably enjoyed the Falernian, they were " projecting " things.

' No one knew it was happening ; but it mattered more than anything else that ever happened at all. Of course this does not mean that all obscure events are important. But it does mean that our estimates of what is important are alarmingly fallacious. . . .

' No one knew what was happening ; more than that—hardly anyone could know. The thing that happened was not deliberately hidden ; it was in its own nature obscure. Yet it was, as Phillips Brooks put it, the meeting place of the hopes and fears of all the years.

' Now—can we get this into our nearly impenetrable heads ? Hardly anything that is recorded in the newspapers is ever of first-rate importance. Because the things of first-rate importance are spiritual events which are known only by their results. Some of them are, of course, really important, but each is always less important than the spiritual event which is the source of them all. The most alert and intrusive of reporters could never have hit upon that stable as the scene of a world-shaking event. When the Baby was become a Man and they executed Him, some report might appear. Probably it would be without comment ; or the Left Wing might regret that lack of a definite policy had involved a promising reformer in futility, while he Right Wing might temper a censure of indifference to the social order with a kindly recognition (now able to be expressed without risk) of an unselfish though misguided spirit, while the Religious Press would insist, after the event, that, of course, persecution was to be deprecated, but this young layman who was for putting the theologians to rights was, after all, impossible. So even if the external event was reported, still it would be true that no one knew what was happening. That Birth, that Life, that Death, could not be recognised by contemporaries for what it was.

'Of course, *we* recognise it now. Oh, do we ? Even on the showing of our own confession we convict ourselves. We say all the great phrases about the thing that happened long ago ; and those phrases declare that it was not a past episode but an eternal fact. It was God Who so died : God, Who is Himself eternal and the eternal principle of all that is. What happened once in that obscure but turbulent corner of the Roman Empire is always happening ; and no one knows it is happening. We can't know how or where ; but we might try to believe that it is going on somewhere.

'We have to go on with the business in hand. Just now it is the war. The result of the war matters as much as anything that gets into the newspapers. But there are things that matter more. The spirit in which we fight matters more than our winning. If we go Nazi and then win, it will be the same for the world as if the Nazis win. But if we can keep charity alive with courage, our victory will be a boon to mankind, and our defeat would be a redemptive agony.

'And even while we fight there may be somewhere a new idea conceived, a baby born, whose effect upon the world will for future historians put even this world conflict in the shade. In 636 A.D. Jerusalem surrendered to the Caliph Omar ; in 635 Oswald had defeated Caedwalla and had summoned Aidan from Iona. On balance, did Christendom gain or lose in those two years ? Perhaps the Chinese war really matters more than the European ; perhaps something that is not a war at all matters more than either. . . .

'Yet there is the precious fact. Though no one knew it was happening, it did happen. The dayspring from on high visited us, to give light to them that sit in darkness and in the shadow of death (in Coventry or Cologne, in

London or Berlin) and to guide our feet where we long to set them—into the way of peace. . . . ' Av. Supplement to No. 61.

THE GOSPEL STORY

The Words and Acts of the Master

The greatest and most sustained piece of exegesis we have from the Archbishop's pen is, of course, the wonderful *Readings in St. John's Gospel*, an attempt to share with any who read it what he found to be his own thoughts as he read the profoundest of all writings. A brilliant Professor, a friend of his and mine, said to me once, that it is not the greatest book the Archbishop wrote, but it is the book of his that it took the greatest man to write. Indeed, no one but William Temple could have written it. Not all, but most, of these extracts on the Life and Teaching of Jesus are from that book :

(The Pharisees') ' demand for evidence was not prompted by a love of truth. They did not wish to believe ; on the contrary they wished not to believe, and they demanded the sign from heaven precisely because they believed that He could not give it ; they were ready to take His refual as a confession of inability and therefore as an excuse for their disbelief. And so their desire for a sign was itself sufficient reason for refusing to give the sign ; for had it been given, their reason would have been convinced while their hearts were still unconverted ; and that is, perhaps, the worst thing that can befall a man. To think our Lord is the revelation of God and to wish He weren't is about as far from discipleship as a man can be. And so our Lord deliberately leaves the Pharisees in unbelief rather than convince them against their will.' J. p. 123.

(Inasmuch.) ' It is Christ Who pines when the poor are hungry ; it is Christ Who is repulsed when strangers are not welcome ; it is Christ Who suffers when rags fail to keep out the cold ; it is Christ Who is in anguish in the long-drawn illness ; it is Christ Who waits behind the prison doors. You come upon one of those who have been broken by the tempests of life, and if you look with the eye of Christian faith and love, he will lift a brow " luminous and imperial from the rags " and you will know that you are standing before the King of kings, the Lord of lords.' J. p. 41.

' *Come is the hour that the Son of Man may be glorified.* The long waiting—first intimated at Cana (ii. 4)—is now ending. Three times this solemn phrase is used—here, at the Last Supper when Judas is gone out (xiii. 31), and in the High-Priestly prayer (xvii. 1). Each time it is in close association with His death. For it is from the Cross that the light of God's love shines forth upon the world in its fullest splendour ; that, therefore, is in a supreme degree the " effulgence of His glory " (Heb. i. 3). Even if the Cross had had no results, it would still be His glory ; for His death is the sealing of His victory. That His body should die was no defeat ; defeat for Him must have taken the form of cursing His enemies or sinking into self-concern. But through all the anguish love was serenely unshaken. To die thus was, in and for His own person, to conquer hate. But it was more than that, it was the means of winning that great multitude of whom the first fruits were now ready to be gathered in. From the Cross He puts forth His might—

' The Man of Sorrows ! And the Cross of Christ
  Is more to us than all His miracles.

' So He goes on at once to lay down the law of life through death—the principle which lies at the heart of the Gospel. Characteristically He finds it first in nature, which illustrates God's laws. At a former crisis He had compared Himself to a Sower, and His proclamation of the Kingdom of God to the scattering of seed, which here and there fails altogether to take root, here and there shows promise and then fails, and only here and there succeeds (St. Mark iv. 3–12). Now He speaks of what happens to the seed which bears fruit. It must first die. It must lose its own identity, that the new plant may spring up. If it did not thus die and lose itself, it remains itself and nothing else ; there can be no fruit. Death is the condition of fuller life.

' Thus in this reply to the Greeks He takes up a point familiar in their mysteries and gives it an added spiritual depth. There is in all Greek thought no appreciation of the excellence of self-sacrifice. It might be necessary, and then those who were capable of it were praiseworthy, and the law of life through death was recognised as a natural fact, and was used in the mysteries as a ground for hope for a future life. But its moral value was not perceived, and no Greek ever dared to say that love is the best thing in life, and that accordingly sacrifice, whereby love expresses itself and strengthens itself, is the best form of action. . . . The mutual sacrifice which expresses mutual love is the most joyous thing in the world. It is the life of Heaven. The Greeks never saw this. . . . Plato never took the step from Justice to Love in his conception of the Idea of Good. This is the point—the vital point—at which the ethics of the Gospel leave the ethics of Greek philosophy far behind.' H. vol. 1, pp. 195, 196.

' *Knowing that the Father had given all things into His hands and that He was come from God and went to God.* The occasion of His action was the dispute among the disciples about precedence ; but it had a deeper motive. He is possessed by a special sense of divine commission and authority. How does He express that sense ? Does He order a throne to be placed that He may receive the homage of His subjects ? No—*He riseth from supper and layeth aside His garments and taking a towel girded Himself ; then He poureth water into the ewer, and began to wash*

*the disciples' feet and to wipe them with the towel with which
He was girded.* So He will display Divine Majesty.

'We rather shrink from this revelation. We are ready,
perhaps, to be humble before God ; but do not want Him
to be humble in His dealings with us. We should like Him,
Who has the right, to glory in His goodness and greatness ;
then we, as we pass from His presence, may be entitled
to pride ourselves on such achievements as distinguish
us above other men.

'But the worship of Jesus Christ makes that impossible
to justify. We worship the Infant in the manger, for Whom
there was no room in the inn. We worship one Who meets
our obedience by rendering to us menial service. So far
as that worship is genuine and complete, pride is eliminated ;
for He Whom we worship is humility itself incarnate.

'The divine humility shows itself in rendering service.
He Who is entitled to claim the service of all His creatures
chooses first to give His service to them. "The Son of Man
came not to receive service but to give it" (St. Mark
x. 45). But man's humility does not begin with the giving
of service ; it begins with the readiness to receive it. For
there can be much pride and condescension in our giving
of service. It is wholesome only when it is offered spontaneously on the impulse of real love ; the conscientious
offer of it is almost sure to "have the nature of sin"
(Article xiii), as almost all virtue has of which the origin
is in our own deliberate wills. For unless the will is perfectly cleansed, its natural or original sin—the sin inherent
in it of acting from the self instead of God as centre—
contaminates all its works. So man's humility shows
itself first in the readiness to receive service from our
fellow-men and supremely from God. To accept service
from men is to acknowledge a measure of dependence
on them. It is well for us to stand on our own feet ; to go
through life in parasitic dependence on others, contributing
nothing, is contemptible ; but those who are doing their

share of the world's work should have no hesitation in
receiving what the love or generosity or pity of others
may offer. The desire " not to be beholden to anybody "
is completely unchristian. Of course, it is equally true that
to take all and offer nothing is even more opposed to the
Christian spirit.

' But it is the service of God which we must above all
be ready to accept. We say in the most familiar of the
Collects, " O God, forasmuch as without Thee we are not
able to please Thee—" our first thought must never be,
" What can I do for God ? " The answer to that is, Nothing. The first thought must always be, " What would God
do for me ? " The answer may be put in many ways ;
one is that He would cleanse me. When I recognise that,
I am both admitting that I need to be cleansed, and acknow-
ledging that I cannot cleanse myself. Moreover, it is to
each singly that the cleansing service is offered, according
to his own stains.' H. vol. ii, pp. 209, 210.

' *Thy life for Me wilt thou lay down? Amen, Amen, I
say to thee the cock shall by no means crow till thou hast
denied Me thrice.* We can imagine a little of the shock
which those words gave to the hearers. To Peter himself
it was such that through all the following scene, though
others spoke, he, the readiest of all to speak, was silent.
His next appearance is at xviii. 10, where he draws his
sword and begins to fight for his Master, and would undoubtedly have then laid down his life, if the Lord had not
stopped the fighting. But great as was the shock to him,
it was little less for his companions, and it is to all of them
that the following words are addressed : *Let not your
hearts be troubled ; believe in God, and believe in Me.*
They were going to fail, and to fail badly. Peter would
deny Him ; and of all it is written that they forsook Him
and fled (St. Mark xiv. 50). The failure must not become
a cause of despair or dismay ; rather let it teach its lesson.
When we fail in our discipleship it is always for one of

two reasons ; either we are not trying to be loyal, or else we are trying in our own strength and find that it is not enough. The former is known to be sinful, but occasions no bewilderment. If we do not try, our lack of success is explained, though our failure to try may well fill us with dismay. The root of that failure, however, is the feebleness of our faith as a settled direction of mind and will. If our habitual faith were stronger we should always try to be loyal. When we try in our own strength and find it in-sufficient, this, too, is evidence of defect in faith. Our faith is strong enough to prompt us to try ; but it is not strong enough to claim the power of God for His service. Until our trust is perfect, we need to supplement our habitual reliance upon God with special acts of trust—probably expressed in secret but conscious prayer—at moments of acute difficulty or temptation.

' Failure, then always proves that faith is insufficient. It should drive us back upon God, forgetfulness of Whose grace has caused the failure. Then every fall into sin can become the occasion for growth in grace. *Let not your hearts be troubled ; trust God, and trust Me.*

' One who so faces his own failures is steadily advancing on the pilgrim's way ; he, like his Master, is going *to the Father.* More than this ; if he is thus travelling the right way at all, he is at home with the Father all the time. *In My Father's house are many resting places. If it were not so, should I have told you that I go to prepare a place for you ? And if I go and prepare a place for you, I come again and will receive you to Myself.*' H. vol. ii, pp. 224–226.

' *If ye love Me, ye will keep My commandments ;* and if we don't we shan't. Let no one deceive himself about that. There is no possibility of meeting His claim upon us, unless we truly love Him. So devotion is prior to obedience itself. I *cannot* obey unless I love and if I am to love I must be with Him Whom I desire to love. Personal com-panionship with Christ is the first requirement, as it was for the disciples in Palestine. If we love Christ, and in whatsoever degree we love Christ, obedience will follow—not the external obedience of the slave who does what he is told, but the gladly given obedience of the friend or the son (xv. 15 ; Rom. viii. 15) whose desire is to give pleasure.

' Our love is cold. It is there but it is feeble. It does not carry us to real obedience. Is there anything that I can do ? No ; there never is, except to hold myself in His presence ; the initiative remains with God. But the Lord, Who knows both the reality and the poverty of our love, will supply our need. *I will ask the Father and He will send you, besides, a Comforter that he may be with you to eternity.*' H. vol. ii, pp. 238, 239.

' *This is the eternal life, to know Thee the only true God, and Whom thou sendest, Jesus Christ.* This knowledge does not earn eternal life ; it is eternal life. Do we hesitate to accept that ? Does it seem to us that just " knowing " a theological truth cannot be an adequate occupation for eternity ? Certainly it could not be. But the word for *know* here is not that which stands for a grasp of truth ; it is that which stands for personal acquaintance. Even in human friendships there is the constant delight of new discoveries by each in the character of the other. Eternity cannot be too long for our finite spirits to advance in knowledge of the infinite God.

' We constantly miss the spiritual value of the greatest religious phrases by failing to recall their true meaning. At one time I was much troubled that the climax of the *Veni Creator* should be

' Teach us to know the Father, Son,
And Thee, of Both, to be but One.

' It seemed to suggest that the ultimate purpose of the coming of the Holy Spirit was to persuade us of the truth of an orthodox formula. But that is mere thoughtlessness. If a man once knows the Spirit within him, the source of all his aspirations after holiness, as indeed the Spirit of Jesus Christ, and if he knows this Spirit of Jesus Christ within himself as none other than the Spirit of the Eternal and Almighty God, what more can he want ? *This is the eternal life.*' H. vol. ii, p. 310.

(Gethsemane.) ' The shadow of His sacrifice drew from Him the sweat like drops of blood and the prayer that He never desired should be answered.' Aw. p. 7.

' All through His life He had shown perfect love to His Father and to men ; always His obedience to His Father was complete. But the love of a boy, perfect in itself, has not the depth of the love of a full-grown man ; and obedience in duties comparatively free from pain has not the heroic quality of obedience unto death. The perfection of the Lord's character at every stage does not wipe out the reality of its growth from one stage to another. We watch the climax of obedience in Him Who, " though He was a son, yet learned obedience through the things which He suffered " ; we watch the climax of love in Him Who, " having loved His own which were in the world, loved them then to the uttermost." For in that climax of His love He put forth in all its fullness His redeeming power, and to be in His companionship in those moments is the way above all others to submit ourselves to His transforming influence.' Ax. p. 14.

' It was not the gross sins such as shock respectable people which sent Jesus to the Cross ; it was the respectable sins which are in the hearts of all of us. It was not the flesh, it was the world, which sought to rid itself of its rightful King—which strongly suggests that worldliness is a more effective enemy of the Kingdom of God than the lusts of the flesh can be. Have we faced the implications of that for our own consciences ? . . . Our deepest sin is always something of which we are unconscious or something of which we are proud. The sinful acts which we remember before God when we confess our sins are no more than the symptoms of our real disease. The very fact that we are able to confess them shows that they are not part of the very stuff of ourselves. But behind them all is that self-centred will, which leads us not only to prefer our way to God's but to claim that our way, just because it is our way, must be God's way also. That is what needs to be changed ; and we cannot change it.' Ax. pp. 15, 16.

' *Jesus, remember me when Thou comest in Thy kingdom.* No other person in all the four Gospels is recorded as having dared to address the Lord by His personal name. Some instinct led all others to use some title such as Lord or Master. The same instinct, or else this custom elsewhere invariable, led some early scribe to alter the text of St. Luke's Gospel so that in our Authorised Version we find it written : " He said to Jesus, Lord, remember me." But that is not the earliest text, which is, as in the Revised Version : " Jesus, remember me."

It is penitence which creates intimacy with Our Lord. No one can know Him intimately who has not realised the sickness of his own soul and obtained healing from the physician of souls. Our virtues do not bring us near to Christ—the gulf between them and His holiness remains unbridgeable. Our science does not bring us near Him, nor our art. Our pain may give us a taste of fellowship with Him, but it is only a taste unless the great creator of intimacy—penitence—is also there. For in my virtue, my art, my knowledge, there is sure to be some pride—probably, indeed, a great deal of pride. But I cannot be proud of sin which is really admitted to be sin. I can be proud of my dare-devilry ; oh yes, and of anything I do to shock respectability. But then I am not admitting to myself that it is sin—only that other people think it is so. When I find something in myself of which I really am ashamed, I cannot at the time be proud of that—though, alas ! I may be proud of my shame at it, and so make this, too, worthless. In straightforward shame at my own meanness there is no pride and no expectation of forgiveness except through trust in the love of Him Who forgives. So it is penitence which brings me in all simplicity to appeal to the sheer goodness and love of God. And we can turn our very sins into blessings if we let them empty us of pride and cast ourselves upon the generosity of God. " We receive the due reward of our sins : Jesus, remember me.' Ax. p. 20.

' Looking down from the Cross He saw His mother and the beloved disciple—Her nephew and His own cousin. Still, as the final agony approaches, He is moved by no self-pity, but by love alone. He does not claim their sympathy, but takes thought for them. He would not have His mother watch the end. So, before the three hours of darkness when Nature provided the counterpart of the darkness in His soul, He bids the beloved disciple lead His mother away to His own home. If, as the story tells us, she went away, that was yet another triumph of love. For her heart must have longed to be near Him till the end. But He would spare her that memory, and she would spare Him the added anguish of knowing that she beheld His agony.

' Will you ask yourself, each one of you who listen, whether when you are in pain or sickness you think of your closest friends chiefly in order to save them trouble and distress ? or do you think of them chiefly as there to meet your needs and do you service ? It is right to accept what love and friendship prompts others to offer us. But we ought not to demand it, or let our suffering become an excuse for exploiting their kindly feelings. As the first word—" Forgive them, they know not what they do "—pierces our complacency by pointing to our unconscious sin ; and as the second word—" To-day thou shalt be with Me in paradise "—tests our penitence by forcing us to consider whether to be with Christ is really our heart's desire, so this word—" Behold, thy son ; behold, thy mother "—sets a standard for our love, in comparison with which it is shewn to be deeply infected with selfishness. Exactly what is best about us has in it elements of that infection from which, if left to ourselves, we can never escape.

' It is good for us to come back and fix our minds upon this one and only expression of perfect love, the love in which self-concern has simply no place at all. This is the essential quality of God. To say that God is love may carry us but a little way if we have not Christ upon the Cross before our mind; it may even be misleading. Ax. p. 24.

' At last He was dying. No one believed on Him. For all His warnings not one soul, except a condemned criminal dying with Him, believed that by His death He was establishing His Kingdom. But if so—then His best appeal was failing. When all other appeals had failed, He still relied on the appeal of His death : " I, if I be lifted up, will draw all men unto Me." He had staked everything upon the faith that God would act—would flash the truth from His dying face into the hearts of His disciples : but God had not acted ; " My God, My God, why hast Thou forsaken Me ? " ' K. p. 23.

' Has not God failed Him ? And if so, what does that mean not only for Himself, but for God ? That is the meaning of this great cry as we can understand it from the outside, as it were. But we know that if we could enter His breaking heart we should find it means more than this. He is dying in apparent failure ; His love is rejected ; yet just because that love remains perfect through its rejection it leads Him to feel as His own the horrible sin which prompts that rejection. By the completeness of His sympathy its burden becomes His own, and He experiences that alienation from God which is the obverse of accepted sin.' Ax. p. 28.

' As St. John records these two words it is evident that

in His mind the Lord gave expression to the agony of
thirst in order that His parched lips and throat might be
moistened so that He could cry aloud the Word of Victory :
" It is Finished." . . . It was the perfecting of love that
was proclaimed in the great cry of victory—" It is Finished."
He had come upon earth to show by life and death the
character of God, Who is Love. As He dedicated Himself
to the last act of sacrifice He had said : " I have glorified
Thee on the earth, finishing the work which Thou gavest
Me to do." Now it is finished. Evil has mustered all its
powers and launched its fiercest assault. But the citadel of
His soul was never surrendered. Through the agony of
the thorns, the nails, the thirst, His love never faltered ;
even through the worst agony of feeling that God Himself
had failed Him, His love never faltered. It remains unshaken, serene, not extinguished but perfected by what it
had to endure.

' Now the world is judged—by the contrast between it
and the perfect love which it could not quench. Now the
victory is won—the only kind of victory with which God
could be content. Now the Kingdom is established—in
the only way in which a Kingdom of the spirit could be
founded.' Ax. pp. 31–34.

THE RESURRECTION

' The sense of failure and desertion was not the real
truth of the matter. " Why hast Thou forsaken Me ? " He
cried. And the answer was the Resurrection.' K. p. 25.

' The Easter message proclaims the triumph of Love over
all these (the enemies of love, which are hatred and malice,
envy and contempt, suspicion and indifference). But it
wins by suffering. If we show love in the face of hatred,
we must not expect to overcome the hatred without suffering. It is by its suffering that love prevails ; that is the

message of Good Friday. But through its suffering it does prevail ; that is the message of Easter Day. The Resurrection proclaims that the only real success is that which is in store for those who love, and will practise a chivalry, even a knight-errantry, which to the world must seem grotesque. We are to trust the untrustworthy and love the unlovely, accepting the misery of betrayals and ingratitude, until our constancy in loving and trusting softens and wins the malignant or suspicious heart.' J. p. 183.

' As she says this, the sorrow comes upon her again in its first fulness, and she turns away from the tomb and its angels. She notices someone standing there ; but she does not recognise Him ; probably she does not look up at Him ; no doubt it is someone who has his own business there. *She turns backward and noticeth Jesus standing, and did not know that it was Jesus.* He too begins, as the angels had begun, by asking the cause of her grief—the first step towards ordinary sympathy : *Woman, why art thou weeping ?* But He knows the real answer, so He adds words which show His understanding. *For whom art thou looking ?* She still does not look up or straight towards Him ; speaking with downcast face and looking away to hide her tears, supposing that He is the gardener she says, *Sir, if thou hast carried Him away, tell me where thou didst put Him and I will take Him.* The word for " carried away " has a suggestion of stealing (xii. 6), but here contains no more than a sad complaint, not a charge. Mary does not answer the question, nor indicate in any way of whom she speaks. That, in her absorption in her grief, seems to her manifest. Her one desire is to find the Lord's Body and take it where friends will pay to it the last tribute of Love and honour.

' *Mary :* the answer is her own name, spoken by a voice she knew. The earlier questions, though spoken by that voice, could not recall the old association. Her name, so spoken, reaches her heart. She turns to face the Speaker.

day will be to say : Yes, surely Christ did expect His
coming almost immediately ; but it was not a *second*
coming. There is nothing in His own language about a
second coming. That all arises from the disciples' failure
to rise to the full height of His teaching. He speaks of the
Coming of the Son of Man. Here, I believe, we have the
true reading of our Lord's own conception of His ministry.'
Aa. pp. 35–38.

THE PERSON OF CHRIST

In his theory of the Person of Christ the Archbishop
started from the ' stratified ' view of the universe already
outlined (p. 107 above) :

' From this it follows that humanity only reveals its true
nature when it is indwelt by what is higher than itself—and
supremely when it is indwelt by the Highest ; and that the
Highest uses what is lower to express Himself and does this
the more adequately as this lower approximates to likeness with Himself, so that of all things known to us human
nature will express Him most perfectly. But if this is so,
and if in Jesus Christ God lived on earth a human life,
then it must be true that in Jesus Christ we shall find two
things. In Jesus Christ we shall find the one adequate
presentation of God—not adequate, of course, to the infinite glory of God in all His attributes, but adequate to every
human need, for it shows us God in terms of our own
experience. But in Jesus Christ we shall find also the one
adequate presentation of Man—not Man as he is apart
from the indwelling of God, but Man as he is in his truest
nature, which is only made actual when man becomes the
means to the self-expression of God.' O. pp. 124, 125.

Attempts to understand how Jesus Christ can be rightly
called God and Man have been hampered by notions of
Deity and humanity arrived at apart from Him :

' Now if in Jesus Christ God lived a human life for the

purpose of inaugurating His Kingdom, that is an event which marks a new stage as truly as the first appearance of life or the first appearance of Man. Therefore, the theory or doctrine of the Person of Christ will not be found by merely stating His nature and works in terms of God and Man, but will involve restating God and Man in terms of the revelation given in Him.' O. p. 127.

' The fact is that most of us are not able to attribute any such meaning to the word " Divine " as will enable us to use that word of Christ, unless we have first seen God in Christ Himself. To ask whether Christ is Divine is to suggest that Christ is an enigma while Deity is a simple and familiar conception. But the truth is the exact opposite to this. We know, if we will open our eyes and look, the life and character of Christ ; but of God we have no clear vision. " No man hath seen God at any time." ' Ar. p. 214.

For example, the revelation of God in Christ is destructive of the two prejudices implied in Arianism :

' The prejudice derived from Hebrew sources is that of the sheer transcendence of God, unbalanced by any doctrine of immanence ; the prejudice derived from Greek sources is that of the divine " apathy " or remoteness from all suffering. The Christian revelation was destined to be destructive of those prejudices ; but they were very deeply rooted, and we are not yet free from their influence, which appears both where they actually persist and in extreme reactions against them.' O. p. 130.

' Until Christianity itself had led to the formation of a tolerably adequate conception of personality, it was inevitable that the problem should be set in terms of Substance or Nature.' O. p. 131.

But the formula of Chalcedon marks the definite failure of all attempts to explain the Incarnation in terms of Essence, Substance, Nature, and the like :

' It is content to reaffirm the fact, but that is all that an authoritative formula ought to do. Interpretations will

vary from age to age, according to the concepts supplied
to the interpreters by current thought. It would be disastrous if there were an official Church explanation of the
Incarnation. Every explanation is bound to be inadequate ;
it will be rare that any explanation is other than positively
misleading. What the Church must safeguard is the fact ;
individual Christians may offer explanations, provided that
in doing so they do not deny or explain away any part of
the fact.' O. p. 134.

' When Life supervenes upon Matter, it does not indeed
lead to any contradiction of the " laws " of physical
chemistry, but it takes direction of the physico-chemical
system ; it asserts priority in the sense that the explanation
of the action of the living thing is sought in the requirements
of its life. The physical system supplies the conditions
sine quibus non ; the life supplies the efficient causation.
So when Mind supervenes upon the living organism, it
takes direction and becomes the cause of the agent's
conduct. We shall expect, therefore, to find that when God
supervenes upon humanity, we do not find a human being
taken into fellowship with God, but God acting through
the conditions supplied by humanity. And this is the
Christian experience of Jesus Christ ; He is spoken of
as a Mediator, but that expression is used, not to signify
one who is raised above humanity by an infusion of deity,
but one in whom deity and humanity are perfectly united.
This is the first point which the early theologians were
concerned about in their insistence that in Christ there is
only one Hypostasis and that this is not human but divine.
The root of this belief is, however, the testimony of Christian
experience that fellowship with Christ is in itself fellowship with God. This testimony coincides with what we are
led to expect by the analogy of the whole Creation. We
may say, then, without any hesitation that Christ is not a
man exalted to perfect participation in the Divine Nature
or Life ; He is God, manifest under the conditions of

humanity. The first disciples had to approach by gradual
stages the realisation of what lay behind the human life
and was finding expression in and through it ; that was
the order of discovery ; but it is not the order of reality.
We see a man's bodily movements first and from them
infer his purpose and character ; but the purpose is prior
and directs the movements. So we see the human life and
infer the divine Person ; but the Person controls and
directs the life. What we find in Christian experience is
witness, not to a Man uniquely inspired, but to God living
a human life.' O. pp. 138, 139.

'Christ's Will, as a subjective function, is, of course, not
the Father's Will ; but the content of the Wills—the Purpose—is the same. Christ is not the Father ; but Christ
and the Father are One. What we see Christ doing and
desiring, that we thereby know the Father does and desires.
He is the Man whose will is united with God's. He is
thus the first-fruits of the Creation—the first response from
the Creation to the love of the Creator. But because He
is this, He is the perfect expression of the Divine in terms
of human life. There are not two Gods, but in Christ we
see God. Christ is identically God ; the whole content
of His being—His thought, feeling, and purpose—is also
that of God. This is the only " substance " of a spiritual
being, for it is all there is of him at all. Thus, in the language
of logicians, formally (as pure subjects) God and Christ
are distinct ; materially (that is in the content of the two
consciousnesses) God and Christ are One and the Same
(Cf. Bosanquet, *Individuality and Value*, p. 272). Clearly,
it is the Logos—the Divine Humanity—that pre-exists.
The " finite centre of consciousness " (Jesus) had a beginning). The Human Affections of Christ are God's Affections ; His Suffering is God's ; His Love is God's ; His
Glory is God's (Cf. the last lines of Browning, *An Epistle*,
also *Saul*, par. xviii).' Ar. pp. 248, 249.

(The Nestorian difficulty.) 'The purpose of the divine

act which is being considered would seem to be twofold—
Revelation and Atónement. For the former, what is
necessary is that Jesus Christ should be truly God and truly
Man ; for the latter what seems to be necessary is that
human experience as conditioned by the sin of men should
become the personal experience of God the Son—not an
object of external observation but of inward feeling (to use
the language of human consciousness). Neither of these
requires that God the Son should be active only in Jesus
of Nazareth during the days of the Incarnation. "The
light that lighteneth every man " did not cease to do so
when He shone in full brilliance in one human Life. Jesus
did not control affairs in Mars, or in China. But God the
Son, Who is the Word of God by Whom, as agent, all
things came to be and apart from Whom no single thing
has come to be, without ceasing His creative and sustain-
ing work, added this to it that He became flesh and dwelt
as in a tabernacle among us, so that as in the old Tabernacle
there dwelt the cloud of the divine glory, so in Him we saw
a glory that shone through Him but found in Him its
perfect and unique expression—" glory as of an only-
begotten Son from a Father." He Who is always God
became also Man—not ceasing to be God the while, for
the Incarnation was effected " not by Conversion of the
Godhead into flesh, but by taking of the Manhood into
God." ' O. p. 140.

' If God the Son lived the life recorded in the Gospels,
then in that life we see, set forth in terms of human experience, the very reality of God the Son. The limitations of
knowledge and power are conditions of the revelation,
without which there would be no revelation *to us* at all ;
but the Person Who lives under those limitations is the
Eternal Son in Whom the life of the Eternal Father goes
forth in creative activity and returns in filial love. The
Incarnation is an episode in the life or being of God the
Son ; but it is not a *mere* episode, it is a *revealing* episode.

There we see what He Who is God's wisdom always is, even more completely than any Kenotic theory allows. This view makes the humiliation and death of Christ " the measure of that love which has throbbed in the divine heart from all eternity." Certain attributes or functions incompatible with humanity are, in this activity of the Eternal Son, not exercised ; but what we see is not any mere parable of the Life of God, not an interval of humiliation between two eternities of glory. It is the divine glory itself.

' As we watch that human Life we do not say : " Ah—but soon He will return to the painless joy of the glory which was His and will be His again." As we watch that Life and, above all that Death we say, " We behold His glory." For if God is most truly known as Love then the glory of God is chiefly seen in the activity of Love.' O. pp. 143, 144.

' We cannot predicate moral progress of God the Son ; we must predicate such progress . . . of Jesus Christ. Therefore, the Will in Him, while always one with, because expressive of, the Will of God, is not merely identical with it. In the struggle with temptation the human will or person is at once manifesting and approximating to the Will of God, until as the Passion approaches and Love is about to be exhibited in the perfection of sacrifice, He prays to be glorified with the eternal glory—which is the perfect sacrifice of perfect love (St. John xvii. 5).

' Consequently, though there is only one Person, one living and energising Being, I should not hesitate to speak of the human personality of Christ. But that personality does not exist side by side with the divine personality ; it is subsumed in it. Will and personality are ideally interchangeable terms ; there are two wills in the Incarnate in the sense that His human nature comes through struggle and effort to an ever deeper union with the Divine in completeness of self-sacrifice. And it is only because there is this real human will or personality that there is here any revelation to humanity of the divine Will. Thus I do not speak of His humanity as impersonal. If we imagine the divine Word withdrawn from Jesus of Nazareth, as the Gnostics believed to have occurred before the Passion, I think that there would be left, not nothing at all, but a man. (The question is so unreal that even to ask it is to make false suggestions ; but I leave the illustration as an expression of my meaning, which is deliberately crude for the sake of pointedness.) Yet this human personality is actually the self-expression of the Eternal Son, so that as we watch the human life we become aware that it is the vehicle of a divine life, and that the human personality (I avoid the phrase " human person," which seems to connote a complete individual more definitely than the phrase " human personality " which I have used) of Jesus Christ is subsumed in the Divine Person of the Creative Word.' O. p. 150.

THE HOLY SPIRIT AND THE CHURCH

The Incarnation was beyond all comparison the most important event in history. Indeed, history, in its full meaning, dates from it :

' Creation and Redemption are, indeed, different ; but they are different aspects of one spiritual fact, which is the activity of the Divine Will, manifesting itself in love through the Creation, and winning from the Creation an answering love. The act whereby this purpose should be accomplished was complete at the Ascension ; all human history from that time onwards is the process of eliciting man's answer. This is still the work of God, but that work is thenceforth within the souls of men rather than on the objective stage.' O. pp. 154, 155.

' When the physical presence of the Lord was withdrawn at the Ascension, there remained on earth as fruit of His

ministry no defined body of doctrine, no fully constituted society with declared aims and methods, but a group of men and women who had loved and trusted Him, and who by their love and trust and conviction of His Resurrection were united to one another. It was in this society that there came the experience of spiritual power, certainly a gift of God, and of inner compulsion to proclaim alike this gift of power and its source in the Life and Death and Resurrection of Jesus their Master. This Society is a veritable Fellowship of the Holy Spirit. It is definable in terms of the Spirit ; and the Spirit is definable in terms of it. To be a Christian is to confess Jesus as Lord, to have the Spirit, to be a member of the Church ; it is all of these or any of them, for no distinction had arisen between them in experience, and none or scarcely any had yet been drawn in thought. Here, in the company of the personal disciples of Jesus, is found an activity of the Divine Spirit so plainly identical with the activity of the same Spirit in Jesus of Nazareth, that St. Paul, who, not having shared the initial training of the others, comes into the society from outside, finds it natural to speak of it as His Body and of its constituent individuals as His limbs or members ! '
O. p. 155.

THE CHURCH

' The ideal Church does not exist and never has existed ; some day, here or elsewhere, it will exist ; meanwhile, its " members " are members also of the " world." The Church only exists perfectly when all its " members " are utterly surrendered to Christ and united to Him. Some such there have been and are. Mostly the members of the Church are still in process of reaching that consummation and have by no means reached it yet. So the Church appears under the guise of a compromising institution ; but the true Church is the Body of Christ, and consists of men *so far as* they are members of that Body. For this reason we ought not in strictness ever to speak of the failure of the Church ; we should speak of the failure of Christians. The failure, which is conspicuous enough in history, is a failure of Christian people to be thoroughly Christian ; in so far as they fail, the Church does not exist on the historic plane ; where it exists, it triumphs, though its triumph, like the triumph of its Head, often appears to the world as failure till the passing of ages brings a true perspective. The true Church does not fail ; but the true Church is still coming slowly into historic existence ; that process is the meaning of History from the Incarnation onwards ; it consists both of the drawing of men and nations into the fellowship of the Holy Spirit, and in the completion of His work upon them in perfecting their surrender to Christ and their union with Him.' O. pp. 167, 168.

' It is quite superstitious to suppose that if Christians proclaimed and lived by the true Gospel, the world would at once accept it. The Church, the true Church which is Christ in His members, may suffer failure for a time. But for the most part what men mean when they speak of the failure of the Church is not really a failure of the Church at all ; it is our failure to be the Church. The Church is the Body of Christ, the organism which moves spontaneously in obedience to His will ; so far as that is not true of us, we are failing to be the Church.' B. p. 70.

' All the old divisions had become negligible. There was one man ; and that man was Christ Jesus. If the will of Christ prevails through a society, for all practical purposes Christ is the only person there. So Christ is the Person of the Church as God is the Person of Jesus Christ.' P. p. 93.

' The vast chaos which for us represents the Church, with its hateful cleavages, its slow-moving machinery, its pedantic antiquarianism (this happens to be peculiarly out of place. The earth will in all probability be habitable for myriads of years yet. If Christianity is the final religion, the Church is still in its infancy. Two thousand years are as two days. The appeal to the " primitive Church " is misleading ; we are the primitive Church), its indifference to much that is fundamental, its age-long ineffectiveness, its abundant capacity for taking the wrong side in moral issues—how can this be described in the language of St. Paul ? His dream was beautiful ; but was it not after all only a dream ? Or if the early Church could be so described, has it not long ago forfeited its splendour ? ' Ar. p. 340.

' The Church militant here and now on earth is a society only half complete, and consisting of members who are also members of the secular and still half-pagan societies which make up Christendom, half pagan, because the standards of our social, commercial, and political life are not even professedly the standards of Christ. Of course it does not realise the ideal of the Apostle's vision, But yet there is in it a life which flows from Christ Himself, and which gives the promise of a completed Church deriving its life from no other source than Him alone. In the sight of God—in the experience of God—that perfected Church is the true reality.' Ar. p. 341.

' We cannot limit the pre-Christian Church to Israel any more than we can deny the presence of Christ's spirit in persons and bodies other than Christians and the Church. Abraham and Isaiah, Socrates and Phidias, Buddha and Confucius, must all be reckoned as, *each in his degree*, a representative and organ of the eternal Church.' Ar. p. 341n.

' There is, and there can be, only one Church. However multiform its organisation, however varied in degree of adequacy its interpretation of the fact of Christ, still in its adherence to that one fact it is one, with a unity not made by its members but by Christ, when in utter loneliness He bore the Cross from Jerusalem to Calvary. . . . The Church on earth is a sacrament, an outward and visible sign of the

Church Universal, and criticism of its outward form no more exhausts its spiritual significance than the geometrical treatment of curves exhausts the significance of their beauty.' Ar. pp. 342, 343.

' The more united the Church becomes, the more necessary is it that individual members should have and exercise freedom of criticism, otherwise there will be no progress.' Ar. p. 353.

THE SPIRIT AND THE FELLOWSHIP

' This (that there is always within us a spark of the Divine Fire) is indeed no discovery of distinctively Christian experience. The mystics have always known it. The discovery is that, when fully known, this " God within my breast " is a source of true fellowship with others. The deepest experience of the Christian is no " flight of the alone to the alone," but a union in God, now known as Love, with Angels and Archangels and all the company of Heaven. The religious soul finds God within itself in all ages. But when God is revealed as Love, this can no longer be a solitary experience ; it becomes an incorporation into the fellowship of all those whom God loves and who in answer are beginning to love Him.' O. p. 169.

' Our fellowship is in the Holy Spirit. Wherever the word Spirit occurs in the New Testament it suggests driving force or energy. The Spirit of God, if God is Love, is a driving energy of love. The Church should be inspired by such an energy of love, wherein all would be united to one another because all are devoted to the purpose of love to all mankind. It is not enough that the members of the Church should have love to one another, nor is it to be expected that unity can be found by reciprocal sacrifice of the sections of the Church to one another. The love that inspires the Body must go out as widely as the love of God, and unity will be found when all sections are united in a common sacrifice for the sake, not of each other, but of the world which Christ died to save. The Holy Spirit is with us now, but we do not give Him free course, and He will not force us, for He is the very Spirit of Love which seeks in answer to itself free love and not coerced obedience. If the Church can learn to give itself to the driving energy of love which is God's gift to it, in the service to which it is then devoted it will find perfect unity within itself.' AA. p. 8.

' Fellowship is valuable in proportion as it brings together to share one another's experience people who are different in antecedents, temperament, and outlook. To take an illustration from the movement towards Christian reunion, it is quite easy to gather into fellowship all those Christians who describe themselves as Evangelicals ; and as far as it goes it is quite a good thing to do, but it is not worth very much. And it is quite easy (psychologically speaking), to gather into fellowship all those Christians who describe themselves as Catholics ; and such fellowships are good as far as they go, but they are not worth very much. The fellowship that is really valuable is one that draws together Catholic and Evangelical on the basis of common loyalty and mutual appreciation. Undenominationalism was a false way of fellowship ; it united men by neglecting their differences. What we need is a unity which is frankly based on differences, where men desire to learn from one another while holding fast to all that they have found true or precious.' Ab. p. 67.

' When men see Catholics and Evangelicals, without any merging of their own distinctive witness, standing as one man in perfect unity for the Holiness of God and the redemption of the world in Jesus Christ ; when they see Christians of different nations standing together as one man in perfect unity for the Kingdom of God ; when they see Christians on both sides of the economic struggle

F—WT

standing together as one man in perfect unity for the Justice of God ; in brief, when men see Christians united because they all seek first " the Kingdom of God and His Justice " ; they will be drawn to the Church to learn its secret. It is the unity of the Church that will convert the world—not the static unity of organisation, though that is necessary in its place, but the dynamic unity of the spirit of reconciliation—even as the Divine Saviour prayed for His disciples—" that they all may be one . . . that the world may believe that Thou hast sent Me." ' Ab. p. 7.

THE REUNION OF CHRISTENDOM

That they may be one.   The Lord is going away.   In the whole world His cause will be represented by this little handful of disciples. If they fall apart, the cause is lost. What is most of all essential is that they be united. We see in the *Acts of the Apostles* in how many ways the infant Church was tempted to disunity—as for example, in the doctrinal difference concerning the authority of the Law for Gentile Christians (Acts xv. 1–29), or the personal difference between Paul and Barnabas concerning John Mark (Acts xv. 36–41). Such division at that stage would have been fatal ; it has been sufficiently disastrous coming later, as it did. So the Lord's Prayer was, and (we cannot doubt) still is, that His disciples may be one.

' But the unity of the Church is precious not only for its utility in strengthening the Church as an evangelistic agent. It is itself in principle the consummation to which all history moves. The purpose of God in Creation was, and is, to fashion a fellowship of free spirits knit together by a love in all its members which answers to the manifested love of God—or, as St. Paul expresses it, to " sum up all things in Christ " (Eph. i. 10). The agent of that purpose is the Church, which is, therefore, called the Body

of Christ, through the activity and self-edifying of which
Christ Himself is " fulfilled " (Eph. i. 23, where we should
read for " the fulness of Him that filleth all in all "—" the
fulness of Him Who, taking things all in all, is being
fulfilled." For the fulfilling of Christ to the " measure of
the stature of His completeness " (Eph. iv. 13) is the meaning of universal history). The unity of the Church is something much more than unity of ecclesiastical structure,
though it cannot be complete without this. It is the love
of God in Christ possessing the hearts of men so as to
unite them in itself—as the Father and the Son are united
in that love of Each for Each which is the Holy Spirit.
The unity which the Lord prays that His disciples may
enjoy is that which is eternally characteristic of the Tri-une
God. It is, therefore, something much more than a means
to any end—even though that end be the evangelisation
of the world ; it is itself the one worthy end of all human
aspiration ; it is the life of heaven. For His prayer is not
only *that they may be one ;* it is *that they may be one as we.*
  ' Before the loftiness of that hope and calling our little
experience of unity and fellowship is humbled to the dust.
Our friendships, our reconciliations, our unity of spirit
in Church gatherings or in missionary conferences—
beautiful as they are, and sometimes even wonderful in
comparison with our habitual life of sectional rivalries
and tensions, yet how poor and petty they appear in the
light of the Lord's longing. Let all of us who are concerned
with Peace Movements or Faith and Order Movements
or " Conversations " with fellow-Christians of other
denominations, take note of the judgement under which we
stand by virtue of the gulf separating the level of our
highest attainment and noblest enterprise, from the " prize
of the call upwards which God gives in Christ Jesus "
(Phil. iii. 14)—*that they may be one as we.*' H. vol. ii, p. 320.
  ' *As Thou, Father, in Me and I in Thee, that they also
may be in us.* Once again we are reminded how trans-

cendent is that theme which alone deserves the name of
Christian unity. We meet in committees and construct
our schemes of union ; in face of the hideous fact of Christian divisions we are driven to this ; but how paltry are
our efforts compared with the call of God ! The way to
the union of Christendom does not lie through committee
rooms, though there is a task of formulation to be done
there. It lies through personal union with the Lord so deep
and real as to be comparable with His union with the
Father. For the prayer is not directly that believers may
be " one " in the Father and the Son, though by a natural
error an early scribe introduced that thought. The prayer
is *that they may be in us.* If we are in the Father and the
Son, we certainly shall be one, and our unity will increase
our effective influence in the world. But it is not our
unity as such that has converting power ; it is our incorporation into the *true Vine* as branches in which the divine
life is flowing. When all believers are truly " in Christ,"
then their witness will have its destined effect—*that the
world may believe that Thou didst send Me.*' H. vol. ii,
p. 327.

' Men notice, with Spinoza, that Christians differ from
others not in faith or love, or any of the fruits of the Spirit,
but only in opinion (*sola opinione*). (Spinoza, *Ep.* lxxiii).'
Ar. p. 351 n.

' We are liable at this time to underestimate the importance of the outward guarantees of order. All the
tendencies of our time are towards unity. There is, therefore, a real risk of achieving unity on easy terms ; and if
that is done, the unity so established will break to pieces
again when the swing of the pendulum comes, and the
tendencies are again towards division. There are some
periods when the Church might maintain its fellowship
without any system of order at all ; there are others when
the only hope of maintaining it is to stand fast by those
elements of Church order which exist to express and

safeguard its nature and purpose, and, therefore, the fellowship of all those who serve that purpose.' B. p. 33.

' In regard to the matter of reunion I find myself quite unable to agree with the proposition that has been advanced that as foundations of the Church faith and order stand on a level. Faith seems to be perfectly indispensable, and about that there must be agreement on the vital points, before union and communion are possible. But that we should agree about any necessary order in the Church for maintaining that seems to me, at any rate, less important and, I am inclined to think, not essential at all. That we must agree what order is in fact to be adopted is plain, for Reunion means the adoption of a common order. But we know quite well that it makes all the difference in the world in our approach to our Free Church brethren whether we say that the Church order which we recommend—and which many of them are after all ready to adopt—is the best for achieving the purpose which the Church has in view and therefore is to be adopted ; or that it is the only one which constitutes the Church as a Church at all and that, therefore, as long as they do not adopt it they forfeit all right to that name. Between these two as methods of approach there is the widest possible difference, though in both cases, as a matter of fact, the result will be that the Church of England will be standing by an order that it has inherited.' Ab. pp. 202, 203.

' As though in preparation for such a time as this, God has been building up a Christian fellowship which now extends into almost every nation, and binds citizens of them all together in true unity and mutual love. No human agency has planned this. It is the result of the great mission-ary enterprise of the last one hundred and fifty years. Neither the missionaries nor those who sent them out were aiming at the creation of a world-wide fellowship in-terpenetrating the nations, bridging the gulfs between them, and supplying the promise of a check to their rivalries.

The aim for nearly the whole period was to preach the Gospel to as many individuals as could be reached so that those who were won to discipleship should be put in the way of eternal salvation. Almost incidentally the great world-fellowship has arisen ; it is the great new fact of our era ; it makes itself apparent from time to time in World Conferences, such as in the last twenty years have been held in Stockholm, Lausanne, Jerusalem, Oxford, Edinburgh, Madras, Amsterdam. . . . We may not hope for the Kingdom of God in its completeness here, but we are to pray for its coming and to live even now as its citizens. And here we find ourselves actually belonging to a fellowship which is an earthly counterpart of that City of God, though many of us are hardly aware of it and all of us are frequently forgetful of it.' The Enthronement at Canterbury. Ae. p. 2.

' We must see our divisions and consider the problems created by our divisions against the background of the paganism of the unconverted, whether overseas or in our own country. At every turn our divisions hinder our service. They blunt our appeal to the general public at home or to the adherents of other religions abroad. They prevent the Government from offering facilities which it could readily offer to a united Church, and does now offer with greater readiness when we can put forward a united claim.' Ae. p. 11.

' The fundamental anomaly is that any two disciples of our Lord should not be in communion with one another. We are so used to this state of things that we seldom pause to appreciate its gravity. I would urge that we try to recover in some measure the horror of divisions among Christians which is evident in St. Paul.' Ae. p. 12.

' We shall remember two facts concerning schism. The first is that while schism is undoubtedly a sinful state, being contrary to the declared purpose of God, yet schism is within the Church, the Body of Christ, and does not effect separation from it as do apostasy and infidelity. The second is that, sinful as schism is, there is no guilt of schism in those who are loyal to the teaching which they have received, still less in those who have been converted from heathenism by missionaries of one or another of our sadly manifold traditions. It is one of the greatest evils of our divisions that they are reproduced in the experience of converts who have no responsibility for them.' Ae. p. 13.

' Many unnecessary difficulties are caused, as I believe, by a readiness to draw negative inferences from positive premises. We have our own grounds of complete assurance that the ministry which we have received is of God. We must at least be very cautious how we conclude that where those grounds of assurance are lacking, the ministry which lacks them is not of God. We should rightly refuse to accept them for ourselves so long as there is no effective intention to heal the breach and restore the universally acknowledged ministry on the basis of what we know as ground of complete assurance. In other words, we cannot in practice recognise what we must regard as irregular ministries, however effective within their own spheres, until there is an operative decision to unite in a way that ends the irregularity. But when that is present ought we not to be ready to recognise during a period of transition what God has blessed and owned until the new rule is generally established and all ministers have been episcopally ordained?' Ae. pp. 20, 21.

' The unity of the Church is essential to the complete discharge of its commission. It is called to give witness to the One God and to the hope of universal fellowship for all mankind in His service. Plainly it cannot do either of these things effectively if it is itself divided and therefore fails to be itself the fellowship into which it calls the various nations and the many sections within the nations. Yet it may be that the difficulty of maintaining and now re-establishing unity is due in part to an over-exclusive emphasis upon the importance of unity as compared with variety ; at any rate it is true that this unity is, in musical terms, one harmony, not of unison. St. Paul's favourite analogy is that of the body, which has one life but many limbs, and all the limbs are different. The life of the body requires every one of them for the fulness of its own expression, and it requires each in its own appropriate place: the loss of any limb imposes a limitation on the body as a whole: the independent activity of any limb is a symptom not of health but of paralysis; and if it were possible that a limb should get into the wrong place, as for example a hand at the end of a leg or a foot at the end of an arm, its utility would be ruined. The unity of the body is a harmony of many parts, each discharging its own function in relation to a single life.' Ae. p. 26.

' In our dealings with one another let us be more eager to understand those who differ from us than either to refute them or to press upon them our own tradition. Our whole manner of speech and conduct, and of course supremely our mode of worship, will inevitably give expression to our own tradition. Wherever there are divisions there is sure to be something of value on both sides. We ought always to be eager to learn the truth which others possess in fuller degree than ourselves, and to learn why some give to various elements in our common belief a greater emphasis than we are accustomed to give. Our temper in conference must be rather that of learners than that of champions.' Ae. p. 29.

' There is no compromise of our distinctive principles involved in our coming together. But there is a choice involved between two different directions of attention. In days when Christianity itself in its fundamental principles is unchallenged it may seem natural to lay most emphasis on the points which distinguish one communion from another. But in days like these when the basic principles of Christianity are widely challenged and in many quarters expressly repudiated, the primary need is for clear and united testimony to Christianity itself. The difference between Catholic and Protestant is very small as compared with the difference between Christian and non-Christian, between those who do and those who do not believe that in Jesus Christ, God hath visited and redeemed His people.

' Our differences remain ; we shall not pretend that they are already resolved into unity or into harmony. But we take our stand on the common faith of Christendom, faith in God, Creator, Redeemer and Sanctifier ; and so standing together we invite men to share that faith and call on all to conform their lives to the principles derived from it.

' As we co-operate with one another, so shall we be ready to welcome into co-operation with us in our particular enterprises all those who share the hope which inspires each enterprise, whether they share our basic faith or not. For there are many who wish to live by the principles which we claim as Christian who are as yet unable to accept the Christian faith in which we are persuaded that those principles are grounded. We shall need their help for the fulfilment of our hopes ; and through their association with us we may lead them to the faith which as yet they have not found.' Ae. pp. 32, 33.

' I regard as a most hopeful sign in the whole situation— the astonishing approximation which has been growing among the theologians of all Christian Communions. Now if that tendency is allowed a little time to develop, we shall find ourselves in a world where the great body of the Christian Communions in this country is really able to stand together, and I am sure that we should encourage in every possible way all that can be done to that end. One of the things which we must do to-day, without the surrender of principles or of our trust, is the removal of whatever may hinder the growth of this agreement." Ae. p. 56.

THE CHURCH OF ENGLAND

It may seem unnecessary to quote from his writings to show that an Archbishop of Canterbury was a convinced and enthusiastic Anglican, but there were timid, unimaginative members of the English Church who feared lest William Temple's friendship for Continental Protestants and English Free Churchmen should lead him to action which might betray the great Anglican heritage. Some extracts will show not only that he was strongly rooted in the Anglican past, but what sort of Anglican he was. As a matter of fact, the Free Churchmen recognised that it was just because he was a convinced Anglican that his friendship for them was significant :

' If it is true that the Church of England contains what for brevity's sake we may call the Catholic and the Evangelical traditions, and, indeed, that this is its most distinctive characteristic, loyalty to the Church must involve an acceptance of this combination and a desire to maintain it. If a man sets out to be loyal to the Catholic tradition, so understood as to rule out all that is distinctive of the Reformation, he cannot also be fully loyal to the Church of England. If a man sets out to be loyal to the Reformation, so understood as to rule out any elements of the Catholic tradition which were not universally maintained by the Reformed Churches, he cannot also be loyal to the Church of England. The Church of England has always bridged the gulf (or sat on the hedge, if you like) that divides " Catholic " and " Protestant " from one another.' AC. pp. 4, 5.

' Critics sometimes say that this (the Anglican method) is tantamount to a declaration that we prefer peace to truth. It would be a fairer account of the Anglican attitude to say that we have learnt from a full experience that nearly always peace is the best way to truth. It is the fact that we commonly put the peace of the Church before our personal convictions ; and, just because we do this, our personal convictions undergo modification from the influence of our fellow-Churchmen, for each side in the controversy learns to value what is·true and wholesome in the contentions of the other.' AC. pp. 7, 8.

' It is not that peace at any price is preferable to truth, but that peace among sincere disciples of Jesus Christ is the first condition for learning fuller truth concerning Him.' AC. pp. 14, 15.

' There remain the two principles which seem to me still fundamental—one, the authority of Scripture . . . and one for which I would rather vary the phrase (the duty of private judgment) now and call it the freedom of the individual religious life. This seems to me quite plainly a characteristic the Church of England deliberately adopted. The whole desire of the Church has been to offer the fulness of God's help to every soul but never to dictate to any soul precisely how that soul may best receive the benefit. It sets a high standard for the individual member. No doubt it involves comparative failure for very many who might, by a more strict and more military discipline, have been led to a fuller use of all means of grace than in fact they practise under the Anglican system. None the less I believe the Church of England did deliberately adopt that attitude, and I believe it did so rightly. For with all the dangers—in fact, humanly speaking, with all the certain loss involved—there is made possible in this way for all members of the Church a fulness of individual apprehension and appropriation which is almost impossible and is certainly discouraged under a system which marks out for men quite clearly their religious duties so that when they have performed these they feel that their duty is done. But that involves us at once in the necessity for a very sharp distinction, or at least a very carefully drawn distinction, between the means and ends of the religious life.' Ab. pp. 201, 202.

' There is . . . the emphasis which the (Lambeth Conference, 1930) Report on the Unity of the Church lays upon the freedom of individual inquiry and individual response to the leading of the Spirit. It is in the combination of these with the maintenance of Catholic order and Evangelical truth that our main difficulties lie. Yet I do not think anyone can doubt that in this emphasis we are true to the heart of the Gospel ; because if there is one thing more conspicuous than any other about the dealing of our Lord with the souls of men it is that always He waited for the response of their hearts and consciences and wills. He wants no unwilling adherents. He offers Himself with all the wealth of divine manifestation to them. They may, if they will, refuse Him ; and if they so choose they are allowed to abide by their choice. And I believe that in that great emphasis upon freedom—what Scott Holland used to call the Anglican " You may " contrasted with the Roman " You must "—we have something which really accords with the genius of the Gospel itself. The characteristic of our Church is to offer to men in all its wealth and fulness the inheritance of the Catholic Church, inviting them to come and take their full share in it, but leaving them always in the last resort to decide.' Ai. pp. 78, 79.

' We shall impoverish our service of the wider fellowship if we let our membership of our own Communion become hesitant or indefinite. Rather we have to make strong the bonds of our own unity, with gratitude for our splendid inheritance, so that we may bring to the universal Church a life strong in faith, in order, in corporate devotion— maintaining all that we have received but recognising also God's gift to His people through traditions other than our own.", Ae. p. 4.

' I like here to recall at his (his own father's) enthronement . . . a quotation from his predecessor and former college tutor, Archibald Campbell Tait—*Nobis Apostolorum vindicamus non honores, sed labores*—We claim for ourselves the Apostles' labours, not their honours.' The Canterbury Enthronement. Ae. p. 5.

' When we go back to the first records of the Church we find neither a Ministry which called people into association with it, nor an undifferentiated fellowship which delegated powers to a Ministry ; but we find a complete Church, with the Apostolate accepted as the focus of administration and authority. When the Lord's earthly ministry was ended, there was found in the world as its fruit and as means of its continuance this Body, in which the distinction of Ministry and Laity is already established. The Apostles were in no sense ministers of the laity ; they were ministers of Christ to the laity, and to the world waiting to be won. They took steps for the perpetuation of the Ministry, and it has descended to ourselves. So when I consecrate a godly and well-learned man to the office and work of a Bishop in the Church of God, I do not act as a representative of the Church, if by that is meant the whole number of contemporary Christians ; but I do act as the ministerial instrument of Christ in His Body the Church. The authority by which I act is His, transmitted to me through His Apostles and those to whom they committed it ; I hold it neither from the Church nor apart from the Church, but from Christ in the Church. I was myself admitted to the episcopate by the twofold succession —succession in office and succession of consecration. The two streams of succession are different from the point where they converged upon me ; but as we trace them back they meet again at some point previous to Gregory who sent Augustine and Vergilius who consecrated him ; and so the double line runs back to apostolic times.

'This authority to consecrate and ordain is itself witness to the continuity of the life of the Church in its unceasing dependence on its Head, Jesus Christ, Who is the same

yesterday and to-day and for ever. Every priest who by
virtue of his Ordination celebrates the Holy Communion
acts not for the congregation there present, not for all
Christian people then living on the earth, but as the organ
of the Body of Christ, the ministerial instrument of Christ
active in and through His Body ; so that though no more
than two or three persons be actually assembled, yet the
congregation at that Holy Communion Service is the
Communion of Saints, with which the persons present, be
they few or many, are there conjoined. Here, therefore, as
in the Incarnation itself, we find the eternal in the midst
of time, the secret of a fellowship against which the gates
of death cannot prevail.

' It is possible to hold such a faith without the sacramental
expression of it in the Apostolic Ministry ; but those who
by God's election have received that Ministry will neither
surrender it nor so hold it as to make difficult the access
of others to it. We hold it as a treasure and a trust. It is
our duty both to safeguard it and to commend it, both to
preserve it for ourselves and our children, and to make
easy the way of entering into participation in it, provided
only that in making our treasure available we do not
dissipate or squander it.' Ae. pp. 24, 25.

' The Catholic doctrine of Apostolic Orders is attacked
on the ground that it implies an unspiritual conception of
God, and has the effect of denying to the individual soul
the freedom of direct and immediate access to the Redeemer.
That is a serious argument ; I think it is mistaken, but I
see how easily the mistake may arise ; and eager as I am
for the organic unity of Christendom, I can easily conceive
that the non-episcopal ministries are, in the providence of
God, a necessary factor in the life of the whole Church
until we are secure against the danger of accepting a magical
interpretation of orders and sacraments.' . Ab. p. 91.

' The ministry has authority in that it is something
which has been received from almost the earliest ages of

the Church, and perhaps from the very beginning of all—something, therefore, which has about it the authority that belongs to the life of the whole body and is beyond any questioning by successive generations as they now come.' Q. p. 38.

'If it be held that episcopal ordination confers a *power* of making sacraments, so that when an episcopally ordained priest celebrates the Eucharist something happens in the world of fact which does not happen on any other condition, then these bodies (the Protestant Free Churches) have no real sacraments. But that is a theory to which I find myself unable to attach any intelligible meaning. It is admitted that the peril to which strong sacramental doctrine is most liable is that of falling into conceptions properly described as magical; and this theory seems to me to lie on the wrong side of the dividing line. What is conferred in Ordination is not the *power* to make sacramental a rite which otherwise would not be such, but *authority* (*potestas*) to administer Sacraments which belong to the Church, and which, therefore, can only be rightly administered by those who hold the Church's commission to do so.' Ai. p. 110.

'I believe that the Heavenly Priesthood of our Lord is active on earth through His (priestly) Body, the Church, and that those called Priests are the organ of this Body for its priestly functions. They become such through the sacramental authorisation conferred in the act of ordination which I regard . . . as conferring " character," that is to say a supernatural quality, a spiritual gift divinely infused, which is in its nature indelible. This character is that of an organ of the Body of Christ, for the exercise of those priestly functions which belong to it belongs to Him ; there is also conferred the divine grace for the exercise of those functions. This is, I think, a coherent view. It accounts for " the impressive, age-long insistence of the East and West that the Eucharist must always be celebrated by a priest " ; provided that " must " is interpreted as meaning " should " rather than " can only." I do not think that there is any authoritative interpretation of *Potestas* as used in the Ordination Service. Until the Reformation there was no occasion to distinguish between Power and Authority in this connexion,—nor indeed was there occasion for this until the movement towards Reunion made it for the first time of practical importance. If I am right in this, either view is consistent with Catholic tradition. When once the question is asked, the fact that Authority, or Constitutional Power, rather than Inherent Force or Ability, is the natural meaning of *Potestas* becomes of some importance.' F. July, 1931.

WORSHIP

' Those who have once heard the call of the Divine Spirit within them to give their lives—St. Paul makes it emphatic by saying their " bodies " (Rom. xii. 1)—as a reasonable return for the love of God towards them, know that they have no right to contentment until this is done. Yet the influence of the world still operates ; and there is no possibility of increasing our self-dedication until it becomes perfect, unless we deliberately and repeatedly turn our minds towards that Love of God, that God of Love, to whom we would be dedicated. This is the place of worship in Christian discipline. If we already love Him and in whatsoever degree we already love Him, we shall desire times when we give our minds and hearts to Him alone. But apart from such a desire, the very obligation to give our lives to God will require a perpetually repeated concentration of attention upon Him in order that we may more and more fulfil our obligation. Throughout our growth as Christians worship is a duty ; as we advance it becomes a delight ; and at all times a true act of worship is the fulfilment—for a moment—of the true destiny of our being. It is this both in momentary actualisation and in promise of future and permanent attainment. It is the one way to that attainment. The command that we should love our neighbour (which is the practical expression of our search for outward or social unity) cannot be fulfilled except so far as we love God. Our " Neighbour " may be for one reason or another the sort of person that we cannot love (so to speak) directly, and the effort to do so will only increase our antagonism. But God, if we once understand Him, we can all love, and so the command to love Him is one that can be obeyed without other conditions being first fulfilled. All can love Him, because for each He is the Life of Life ; by Him I live ; by Him I came to be ; by Him I aspire, so far as I aspire at all, to better things. If I realise Him, I must love Him. So I may fitly be commanded to love Him ; and from this I shall go on to love my neighbour, for God's sake if not yet for his own. But as I become more perfectly united to God, I begin to love my neighbour as God loves Him, that is for himself, or for the good thing that he at least can be and can bring into being. In the perpetual return of our hearts and minds to God in worship we both enjoy a foretaste of our perfect happiness, and find the renewal of spiritual strength by which we do the work which fits us for it.' O. pp. 230, 231.

' If the idea of God with which you fill your mind is that of a proud Being, or capricious, or vindictive, your own character will be more marked by pride or caprice or vindictiveness in proportion as your worship is genuine and deep. . . . Men like Cicero could join in mumbo-jumbo rites before images of heathen deities without suffering much harm, because they did not believe in it.' B. p. 3.

' What is required by a man's duty, and therefore by his duty to God, is that every man should devote his energies to the task he has in hand with complete concentration of thought and will ; whatever is man's task in life, he must give himself to it in the hours allotted to it. He must not at that moment be wrapped in a mystic trance ; if he is he will only do his work badly. For that trance there is another time, and to let it intrude upon the ordinary duties of life is a disproportion ; indeed, so far as it goes, it is sin. It is our duty to do the allotted task, and in the Decalogue the commandment which deals with this subject is quite as explicit in saying " six days shalt thou labour " as in saying that the seventh day is to be kept holy. What that means is that for a great part of our time our duty to God requires that we should withdraw our attention from Him. It is not our duty to be consciously and positively thinking about God all day long, because He Himself has given us our task to perform, and our duty in the performance of that task is to do it to the best of our ability. But, just because that is true, we cannot perform our ordinary work as duty to God, unless we are also giving times—and abundant times—in which we bring our minds back to the contemplation of Him. . . .

' What is it that is significant, if that is so, in the present tendency towards the secularisation of Sunday? It is exactly that these points of time on which we rely for the perpetual maintenance and renewal of our remembrance of our creatureship, of our utter dependence on God, and of our highest destiny being fellowship with Him, may be gradually whittled away until, while there is no open denial of these truths, there is in the practice of life no effective memory of them. That is the risk and danger. It is a real threat to the vitality of religion as a force alike in individual and in public life.' F. Diocesan Conference Address, May, 1930.

' There is the critic who says, " Do you really mean to tell me that what God wants people to do is to come together into buildings and sing little songs about Him ? " There is nothing so easy in giving a description of our activities in worship as to make them seem ridiculous because plainly they are inadequate to what they represent. Of course it is true that God does not want us literally to come together to sing hymns about Him. What He does desire, and desires for our sakes, is that we should come and truly open our hearts to Him, acknowledge our dependence upon Him, fix our thoughts upon Him for another period in the utmost concentration we can compass in order that He may fully take possession of us and use us. And the means by which we do that will always seem meaningless to those who do not understand and know what lies behind it. . . . It is precisely the shutting out of all that might stand between the soul and God, unveiling and baring the heart before Him in order that we may with unveiled face reflect as in a mirror the glory of the Lord.' F. May, 1930.

Again and again he gave his description of worship, in slightly different words. One has been quoted above Perhaps the most successful of these definitions is the following :

' What worship means is the submission of the whole being to the object of worship. It is the opening of the heart to receive the love of God ; it is the subjection of conscience to be directed by Him ; it is the declaration of need to be fulfilled by Him ; it is the subjection of desire to be controlled by Him ; and as the result of all these together, it is the surrender of will to be used by Him. It is the total giving of self. . . . But it is evident that if this is what worship means, only the perfection alike of reality and of goodness can claim it ; and to offer worship, in the true sense of worship, to anything other than the true God must be at least the most disastrous, if it is not—as it probably is—the most wicked, of all possible human activities.' AD. p. 15.

' The act of worship . . . like all other human acts, must at least have physical expression, and is so far always sacramental. Moreover, it is generally assumed that if the worship is silent, that silence is charged with the power of the Spirit ; if forms of words are used, they are words prescribed by the Church which was guided by the Spirit in choosing them ; if free prayer is used, the speaker is guided by the Spirit in his utterance ; if the sermon is a part of the service, the preacher is taught by the Spirit. So we cannot say that in other worship the outward form expresses and conveys *our* thought or desire while in a sacramental rite the outward form expresses and conveys the power of God. In fundamental principle there is no difference whatever between specific sacraments and any other mode of worship. . . . But in the sacraments commonly so called everything combines to insist on the priority of the divine action. We only benefit in so far as we are actively receptive ; but the initiative is not only ultimately but manifestly and avowedly with God.' O. p. 233.

' The principle of the sacraments of the Church is one which pervades all experience. This use of the material as a vehicle of the spiritual is not unique, but is a special instance of what is everywhere taking place. Thus the sacraments reveal, or at least illustrate the true relationship between spirit and matter. You do not become more spiritual, in the Christian sense, by paying less and less attention to the material, but taking care that the spiritual controls the material and that the spiritual more and more expresses the material.' AE. p. 5.

' Why should there be special sacraments at all ? Why not be content to remember with thanksgiving the presence of God as mediated through Nature, or as revealed in the Inner Light at the core of every soul ? The answer I should give to this is that we need sacraments to get away from self-concern. What matters to me about Baptism is that therein, quite apart from anything I did or could do, " I was made a member of Christ, the child of God, and an inheritor of the Kingdom of Heaven." I may become a palsied member, a disobedient child, a disinherited heir.

But what matters is that I do not make myself either member, child, or inheritor. No doubt it is most important that I should give my will to Christ, and in that sense choose, or decide, for Him. But it is much more important and primary that He has chosen me. " Ye did not choose Me, but I chose you." And it is only because of His Spirit moving within me and at work upon me that I am able to choose Him. It is no merit of mine that I was born in a Christian country, or that I ever heard the Gospel. To have that privilege is to be " elect " ; and no one can " elect " himself.' AE. p. 6.

' In truth the Church is itself the permanent sacrament ; it is an organised society possessed (though not always availing itself) of a supernatural life—the life of God— which united humanity with itself in Jesus Christ. But all of this again was only possible because the universe itself is an organ of God's self-expression. Thus we have the following background of the sacramental worship of the Church : the universe is the fundamental sacrament, and taken in its entirety (when of course it includes the Incarna- tion and the Atonement) is the perfect sacrament exten- sively ; but it only becomes this, so far as our world and human history are concerned, because within it and determining its course is the Incarnation, which is the perfect sacrament intensively—the perfect expression in a moment of what is also perfectly expressed in everlasting Time, the Will of God ; resulting from the Incarnation we find the " Spirit-bearing Body," which is not actually a perfect sacrament, because its members are not utterly surrendered to the spirit within it, but none the less lives by the Life which came fully into the world in Christ ; as part of the life of this Body we find certain specific sacraments or sacramental acts.' O. p. 234.

' You notice this result in any of the thinkers who deny the existence of matter ; a nemesis follows, in that they proceed to set up a materialistic conception of spirit, and

leave themselves after all with what is really a materialistic
universe. When you find such an argument as this : " If
God is Spirit, and God is everywhere, there is no room for
matter," you know that the author had a purely materialistic conception of spirit. Spirit does not occupy space.
You may have spirit everywhere and the whole universe
open for material existence as well. There is no contradiction. Spirit does not manifest itself through the occupation
of space, but in thinking and feeling, in loving and hating ;
and these things don't take up any room. You can have
any number of stars in a universe in which people love one
another.' P. pp. 47, 48.

THE HOLY COMMUNION

In 1923, on April 27th, William Temple spoke in the
House of Bishops in support of the motion that the Prayer
Book Revision Measure be given general approval :

' For us there is only one sacrifice ; it is the sacrifice of
Christ. . . . But Christ as Man is not merely an individual.
. . . His sacrifice set forth at a moment of time on Calvary
is in truth the inner life of the perpetual sacrifice which
consists in the coming of mankind into perfect obedience
to God. This is not the time to dwell on the difficult but
absolutely necessary doctrine that Christ is Humanity.
But this doctrine pervades the Pauline Epistles, and is
expressed particularly in the thought of the Church as the
Body of Christ, growing to completeness as nations and
individuals are brought into it. And it is noticeable that
the same term is used here as of the consecrated Bread—
the term Body. Each is the Body of Christ, because each
is the medium through which He Himself becomes effective.

' The sacrifice, then, is always Christ ; and first as offered
under the form of the sacramental elements. He is not
locally in the elements. Even the classical exponent of

Transubstantiation, St. Thomas Aquinas, denies that Christ is locally in the Sacrament. (*Corpus Christi non est in hoc sacramento sicut in loco*, S. T. iii. Q. lxxvi. A. v.) But the Sacrament is a medium of His Presence to us ; and that Presence, given under such a medium as to show that it is granted in order that it may be received (for bread and wine are food and drink), incorporates us into His Body, so that in the power of the eternal sacrifice we may take our allotted share therein, " filling up what remains of His sufferings, for His Body's sake, which is the Church."

' So there is one sacrifice, achieved in fact and power on Calvary, represented in the breaking of the bread whereby He taught us the meaning of Calvary, reproduced in our self-dedication and our life of practical service in the world resulting therefrom, consummated in the final coming of the Kingdom. " We do show forth the Lord's death till He come." The Death and the Coming are the initial and the crowning moments of the triumphant sacrifice.

' What sacrifice do we offer ? There is only one. Is it of the elements or of ourselves ? It is neither separately, but always of both—and the reality is something more even than this. The Body, which by the hand of the Priest the Church breaks and gives, is the Church itself, which is " the Messiah building Himself up into His fulness." Our offering of ourselves is not an act of our own motion ; it is but our self-surrender to the movement in humanity of the sacrifice of Christ the Universal Man.' Ac. June, 1923.

' The Present . . . is that which is directly apprehensible. . . . Through the consecrated elements we find Christ specially apprehensible so that though He is not personally localised, He is accessible by what is local. The elements come by the act of Consecration to be the vehicle to us of His Human Nature and Life. That is now their value, and therefore their true " substance." (Perhaps it is really enough to say that Present is the opposite of

Absent. . . .   The doctrine of the Real Presence is the assertion that by means of the consecrated elements Christ is really and fully accessible to us and apprehensible by us.)   There is nothing here of magic or even of miracle, if-miracle means a fact for which other experience offers no analogy.   But there is here something possessed of as high a dignity as any miracle could ever be—a clear manifestation of the principle which informs the whole universe, the utilisation of lower grades of being for the purpose of the higher, even of the highest.'   O. p. 240.

' No doubt Christ is always and everywhere accessible ; and He is always the same.   Therefore it is possible to make a " spiritual communion " which is in every way as real as a sacramental communion.   Where Christ is at all, there (I hold) He is altogether.   To say that His Divinity is present elsewhere but His Humanity only in the Eucharist seems to me mythology, and nonsense at that. Everywhere and always we can have full communion with Him.   But He has provided a way perfectly suited to our needs and capabilities, and if we neglect this our presumption in doing so will hinder our communion by other means.'   O. p. 241 and n.

' The reality of our communion with Christ and in Him with one another is the increase of love in our hearts.   If a man goes out from his Communion to love and serve men better he has received the Real Presence.   If he feels every thrill and tremor of devotion, but goes out as selfish as before, he has not received it.   It was offered but he did not receive it. . . .

' The energy which I acquire from food and drink I may use for selfishness or for love, for gain or for service ; let there then be some food—common in its own type— which by association with the self-sacrifice of Christ reminds me of the only right I have to live at all, which is that I may live for God.'   O. pp. 242, 243.

' It is the family meal, where the children gather round

the Table to receive what their Father gives them. And
what He gives, through His incarnate Son, is His own
nature ; in other words, it is love. But if we receive love,
of course we become more loving ; we are more closely
united with our brother men ; for love is the capacity
for, and joy in, the union of spirits.' B. p. 49.

PRAYER

The fullest statement on prayer in the Archbishop's
writings occurs in the second volume of the *Readings in
St. John's Gospel*, in an appendix to the meditations on
chapter xvi.

' In chapter xvi we find the culmination of the Lord's
teaching on Prayer ; in chapter xvii we have His own
prayer of self-consecration offered as Priest-Victim, Victim-
Priest. It is worth while to pause for a moment and consider His teaching on Prayer as a whole.

' First must be put the fundamental principle that God
is perfect love and wisdom ; He has no need that we should
tell Him of our wants or desires ; He knows what is for
our good better than we do ourselves, and it is always His
will to give it ; "Your Father knoweth what things ye
have need of before ye ask Him" (St. Matt. vi. 8). Consequently we must not in prayer have any thought of
suggesting to God what was not already in His mind—
less of changing His mind or purpose.

' But what things are good for us may depend on our
spiritual state. Food which is wholesome and nourishing
for those who are in good health may be lethal poison to
any who are in high fever. The worst of all diseases of the
soul is detachment from God, whether by ignorance or
neglect. If all our wants are supplied while we have no
thought of God, this may confirm us in our detachment
from Him, and so the things that should have been for

our wealth are unto us an occasion of falling (Ps. lxix. 22).
Consequently the question whether what is normally a
blessing, such as deliverance from the enticement of some
temptation, will be in actual fact a blessing to me, may often
depend on whether or not I recognise God as the source
of all good things. So the first requirement in prayer is
that we trust to God for all blessing.

' Our Lord, according to His custom, states this in its
place without qualification and without reserve. He goes
to the greatest possible length in the demand that as we
pray we shall believe that God will hear and answer, and
in the promise that God will then grant our petitions.
Many sayings might be quoted ; one is sufficient : " All
things whatsoever ye pray and ask for, believe that ye have
received them and ye shall have them " (St. Mark xi. 24).

The next requirement is apparently inconsistent with
this ; for this next requirement is that we should persevere
in prayer in spite of disappointment. We are to be sure
that God will grant our prayers ; and when He does not,
we are to go on praying. Our Lord gives His teaching
about perseverance in two parables which belong to that
well-marked group of parables whose point is that the
comparison fails. For in these the Lord illustrates God's
dealing with us, or our duty before God, by reference to
human actions which are not morally admirable. Such are,
evidently, the parable of the Unjust Steward (St. Luke
xvi. 1–9) and, as I think, the parable of the Labourers in the
Vineyard (St. Matt. xx. 1–16). The duty of perseverance
in prayer is urged upon us in the parables of the Importun-
ate Friend (St. Luke xi. 5–10) and of the Unjust Judge
(St. Luke xviii. 1–8). We know that God does not grant
petitions in order to rid Himself of the nuisance which we
become by our persistence ; His choice of a parallel so
completely inapposite is a challenge to us to seek the real
reason why God may make long delay and then grant our
request.

surprised that their request was selfish in the worst sense—
it was for something by gaining which they would keep
others out of it. To such a prayer for selfish advantage
there is and can be only one answer : Can you share My
sacrifice ? (St. Mark x. 35–38).

' The essence of prayer is to seek how we may share that
sacrifice. It finds its fullest expression in the Eucharist
where we offer ourselves to Christ that He may unite us
to Himself in His perfect self-offering to the Father—that
self-offering to which He dedicated Himself in the great
prayer which St. John now calls us to hear with adoring
wonder . . . what is, perhaps, the most sacred passage in
the four Gospels (St. John xvii).'[1] H. vol. ii, pp. 302–307.

To this it will be fitting to add other statements of his
on prayer, and, first, as he would wish, his teaching on
Intercession.

' Prayer is the giving out of our love, in communion
with the love of God, towards those for whom we pray ;
but if there is no love in us for those for whom we are
saying prayers, there will be no true prayer said. . . . Yet
where there is very little love, prayer can increase it ; and
by expressing in our prayer the very little love we have, it
may be, for example, for the unconverted heathen, we shall
come to feel more love for them.' Q. p. 152.

' God is love ; and the love from which prayer springs
is the Holy Ghost at work in our hearts. The Christian can
never think of love as a mere sentiment or state of feeling ;
it is a power ; it is the supreme power of the world. That
it should be generally realised as this is the first condition
of human welfare. And one way to this is prayer, which
expresses and so increases the love that is to prevail over
all other forces.' B. p. 40.

Prayers for the dead have been, and what is called the
invocation of saints still is, almost a party slogan in the

[1] In 1914 he had called that prayer "the most sacred words in all the
world . . . . ." K. p. 58.

Church. It is characteristic of William Temple that he spoke and wrote of these things with perfect naturalness, and therefore persuasiveness :

'Let us pray for those whom we know and love who have passed on to the other life. The objection to prayers for the dead rests on two assumptions, one of them unfounded and the other definitely false. The first is the assumption that at death all is irrevocably settled ; whatever be the state of the soul at that moment, in that state it must unalterably remain. Neither in revelation nor in reason is there a shred of evidence for this once prevalent delusion. We cannot doubt that growth in grace and power and love continues after death. The other assumption which leads men to object to prayers for the dead is the belief that we should only pray for such blessings as we fear may not be granted unless we pray for them. But this is flatly contradictory to the teaching of Christ. We are to pray for all good things because it is our Father's will to give them, and we should acknowledge that we receive all good things at His hand. We do not pray for them because God will otherwise neglect them. We pray for them because we know He loves and cares for them, and we claim the privilege of uniting our love for them with God's.

'But do not be content to pray for them. Let us also ask them to pray for us. In such prayers while they lived on earth they both displayed and consecrated their love towards us. Doubtless that ministry of love continues ; but let us seek it, ask for it, claim it. It is in the mutual service of prayer, our prayer for them and theirs for us, that we come closest to them. For our fellowship with them is " in Christ," and we find them when we seek them in His Name.' An All Saints' Day sermon in Westminster Abbey, 1919. J. pp. 78, 79.

'There is always a certain paradox about prayer. Only by prayer can we win certain blessings ; yet if it is chiefly for the sake of the blessings that we pray, our prayers are poor prayers, and may not merit the blessings.' F. Oct. 1931.

' Thanksgiving is a far more important element in the devotional life than many people accustomed to say their prayers have recognised. When we pray for something not yet obtained, our own wish, as well as our recognition of God's supremacy and goodness, plays a large part in the petition. There is always a chance that we shall be trying to use God for the fulfilment of our purposes. But when we have received what we desired, to turn back to God and give Him thanks is a sheer recognition of His goodness and supremacy. It is a far more selfless thing than petition for those things in which our own desires are actively engaged. There can, of course, be completely unselfish petition in the shape of intercession, and the more of it that we can practise, the better ; but our own prayers are of necessity largely coloured by our passionate concern for the success of our cause and the safety of our friends. There is nothing in the least wrong about all this. It is merely natural and necessary. But we can to some extent see how far we have allowed this self-centred concern to become uppermost if we watch how ready we are to pause and give thanks when those blessings for which we have prayed are granted—or other blessings of which we have never thought. Christian thanksgiving, of course, must always be more than a verbal expression of gratitude. It must always take the form of fresh dedication that we may show forth God's praise " not only with our lips, but in our lives." ' G. October, 1944.

' I would remind you, merely to clear away a common misunderstanding, that if you are praying for growth in spiritual goodness, the answer is pretty certain to take the form of your having or seeing opportunities for practising those virtues to which you have hitherto been blind, or in which you had been lacking—as in the case of the lady who prayed for patience only to have her prayer answered by being provided with an ill-tempered cook. We cannot have patience except in the exercise of it ; and, therefore, to pray for patience is to ask, in effect, that your life may be for a little while rather specially irritating ! ' A. p. 27.

' The truly effective prayer, the prayer that makes a difference in practice in the world is the prayer that is offered by the man who does not primarily care about the difference that he makes, but primarily cares about the glory of God. . . . God's will for us may be that we should try even though we fail. . . . I may be going to carry out His purpose precisely through my failure, the way I bear it, and the lessons men learn from it.' A.

' We can never rightly pray against others. In the war we could rightly pray for victory only so far as we sincerely believed that this was good for the Germans. At any time in those dreadful years (of the first world war) an English-man and a German could have knelt side by side praying the Lord's Prayer ; and they would have meant exactly the same thing. This is always true of Christian prayer.' B. p. 41.

'Above all, do not spend the whole time of prayer talking yourself. Bring the needs of the world, and the problems of your life, before God ; then leave them with Him and wait for a while in silence not only from speech, but as far as possible from thought, just desiring with all your force that in these things God's will may be done, and resting in the quiet assurance of His love and power. There is no limit to what God will do by means of us if we train ourselves to trust Him enough.' Ac. Feb. 1925.

It is fitting that these extracts from the Archbishop's teaching on prayer should be illustrated by examples of some of the prayers he wrote :

PRAYERS

Three Prayers written for his wife at the time of her mother's death.

' O God, our loving Father, we pray Thee to keep us ever close to Thyself, that we may find in Thy love our strength and our peace ; through Jesus Christ our Lord—Amen.'

' Almighty Father, in Whose hands are our lives, we commend ourselves to the keeping of Thy love. In Thy will is our peace. In life or in death, in this world and the next, uphold us that we may put our trust in Thee ; through Jesus Christ our Lord.'

' O Lord our God, from Whom neither life nor death can separate those who trust in Thy love, and Whose love holds in its embrace Thy children in this world and in the next, so unite us to Thyself that in fellowship with Thee we may be always united to our loved ones whether here or there : give us courage, constancy and hope ; through Him Who died and was buried and rose again for us, Jesus Christ our Lord.'

A Prayer for Christmas—For service at the Crib in York Minster.

' We pray Thee, O Lord, to purify our hearts that they may be worthy to become Thy dwelling place. Let us never fail to find room for Thee, but come and abide in us that we also may abide in Thee—Who as at this time wast born into the world for us and dost live and reign King of kings and Lord of lords now and evermore.'

' O Almighty God, Who hast entrusted this earth unto the children of men, and through Thy Son Jesus Christ

G—WT

called us unto a heavenly citizenship : grant us, we humbly beseech Thee, such shame and repentance for the disorder and injustice and cruelty which are among us, that fleeing unto Thee for pardon and for grace we may henceforth set ourselves to establish that city which has justice for its foundation and love for its law, whereof Thou art the Architect and Maker ; through the same Lord Jesus Christ, Thy Son, our Saviour.' I. p. 23.

' O Blessed Saviour, Hero of heroes and Prince of Peace, call us and all men into fellowship with Thee, that sharing Thy perfect union with the Father we may know that peace which passeth understanding and therein find guardianship of heart and thought in Thee. For we are weak and selfish and proud. Even our suffering leaves us selfish still. By Thine Agony and Bloody Sweat, by Thy Cross and Passion, by Thy glorious Resurrection and Ascension, give us the Life Divine, the Life of Love, which is alone the very bond of Peace.' J. p. 196.

' O Jesus, Master and Lord, pour into our hearts Thine own heroic Love, that being filled with Love we may know the Love which passeth knowledge, and live in the unknown power of Love to win men to trust in Love, to the glory of God Who is Love. Amen.' J. p. 243.

' Almighty God, Who gavest Thine only begotten Son Jesus Christ to die for the sins of the whole world, have mercy on all who are in temptation and upon all who through weakness or wilfulness fall into sin ; make known to them Thy gracious love and so teach them the evil of hatred and malice, of envy and contempt, of lust and greed, that, turning to Thee for help they may be led into fellowship with Thee and obedience to Thy will, through Jesus Christ our Lord.'

' Almighty and eternal God, so draw our hearts to Thee, so guide our minds, so fill our imaginations, so control our wills, that we may be wholly Thine, utterly dedicated unto Thee ; and then use us, we pray Thee, as Thou wilt, but always to Thy glory and the welfare of Thy people, through our Lord and Saviour, Jesus Christ.' A.

' O Lord, Jesus Christ, true Word and Revelation of the Eternal Father : come, we beseech Thee, take possession of our hearts and reign where Thou hast right to reign. So fill our minds with the thought and our imaginations with the picture of Thy love that there may be in us no room for any desire discordant with Thy holy will. Cleanse us, we pray Thee, of all that makes us deaf to Thy call or slow to obey it, Who with the Father and the Holy Spirit, livest and reignest, one God for ever and ever.' A.

' O blessed Jesus, Who knowest the impurity of our affection, the narrowness of our sympathy, and the coldness of our love, take possession of our souls and fill our minds with the image of Thyself ; break the stubbornness of our selfish wills and mould us in the likeness of Thine unchanging love, O Thou Who only could, our Saviour, our Lord and our God.' C. p. 83.

' O loving Saviour, we would linger by Thy Cross, that the light of Thy perfect love may shine into the secret places of our souls, showing what is vile there so that it may shrink away and nurturing whatever there is pure or lovely or of good report, so that beholding Thee we may become more like Thee, Thou Revealer of God to men, Thou Guide of men to God.' Ax. p. 17.

' Help us, dear Lord, to see ourselves as Thou seest us ; help us, in shame for what we are, to cast ourselves in trust upon Thy love ; speak to us the word of pardon, for our trust is not in any virtue or wisdom of our own, but only in the mercy and love of God which Thou hast shown to us in Thy Life and in Thy Death, Jesus, our Lord and our God.' Ax. p. 21.

' O Loving Jesus, by the strength and purity of Thy love, cleanse our love of every trace of selfishness, that when we love we may love truly and loving truly may love more widely, till at length we love Thee with all our hearts and

all our neighbours for Thy sake, in Whom by the
energy of the eternal Spirit is shown to us the love of the
eternal Father, God blessed for ever and ever.

' Lord Jesus Christ, Who didst for me endure the horror
of deep darkness, teach me by the depth of Thine agony
the vileness of my sin, and so bind me to Thyself in bonds
of gratitude and love that I may be united with Thee in
Thy perfect sacrifice, my Saviour, my Lord and my God.'
Ax. p. 30.

' Father, into Thy hands we commend our country and
its cause ;   into Thy hands we commend ourselves, our
souls and bodies ;   into Thy hands we commend our dear
ones, near or far away ;   in the companionship of Thy
Son Jesus Christ and in the power of His Spirit, we commend
into Thy hands all we have and all we are ; Abba, Father,
into Thy hands.'   Ax. p. 39.

' O Lord Jesus Christ, Who didst pray for Thy disciples
that they might be one, even as Thou art one with the
Father :   Draw us to Thyself, that in common love and
obedience to Thee we may be united to one another, in
the fellowship of the one Spirit, that the world may believe
that Thou art Lord, to the glory of God the Father.'
D. p. 95.

' O God, the King of Righteousness, lead us, we pray
Thee, in the ways of justice and of peace : inspire us to
break down all tyranny and oppression, to gain for every
man his due reward and from every man his due service ;
that each may live for all, and all may care for each, in
the Name of Jesus Christ.'   D. p. 161.

' O God our Father, Who hast sent Thy Son to be our
Saviour : Renew in us day by day the power of Thy Holy
Spirit ;   that with knowledge and zeal, with courage and
hope, we may strive manfully in Thy service :   may He
keep our vision clear, our aspiration high, our purpose
firm, and our sympathy wide ; that we may live as faithful
soldiers and servants of our Lord Jesus Christ.' D. p. 255.

' Most loving Saviour, we would abide in Thee : Make our hearts Thy dwelling-place ; fill our minds with the thought and our imaginations with the picture of Thy love ; take away whatever in us of selfishness or weakness hinders our hearing or obeying Thy call ; teach us day by day to live closer to Thy side, which was pierced that we might live.' D. p. 256.

' O dearest Saviour, Thou Word and Revelation of the Father ; purge us by the power of Thy love from pride and prejudice, from boasting over the past and ambition for the future ; take our lives and our school into Thine own hands and so use us in prosperity, in poverty or through death that, so far as lies in us, Thy kingdom may come and Thy will be done in earth as it is in heaven.' C. p. 312.

' And the God of all love, Who is the source of our affection for each other, take our friendships formed here into His own keeping, that they may continue and increase throughout life and beyond it.' C.

' O Lord Jesus Christ, Thou Word of God, Creator and Redeemer, possess our mind and conscience, our heart and imagination by Thine indwelling Spirit, that we and all men, being purged of pride, may find and rest in that love which is Thy very self. Amen.' R.

' Let us pray for industrial peace and goodwill.

' Let us pray that all men may learn to seek first the Kingdom of God and His righteousness, caring for justice more than for gain and for fellowship more than for domination.

' Let us pray that all may have the courage and the energy to think for themselves strongly and clearly, and to seek for the truth and follow it whatever it may cost.

' Let us pray for deliverance from prejudice and for a desire to appreciate what is just and true in the opinions of those who differ from us.

' Let us pray that all may have the faith to believe that whatever is right is always possible, and that what is according to the mind of Christ is upheld by the limitless resources of omnipotence.

' Let us pray that in ourselves and in others suspicion may give place to trust, and bitterness to goodwill ; and that we may all become trustworthy, whether we work with hand or brain.

' Let us pray that God will grant peace in our time, and give us abundantly of His Holy Spirit, whose fruits are love and joy and peace.' Ac. May, 1921.

Towards the end of 1931, when the world was at the very trough of the worst economic depression ever known, the two Archbishops, with the approval of the King, appointed Sunday, January 3rd, as a Day of National Prayer. In due course a Form for use in churches on that day was published. It is common form, of course, to speak lightly or severely of such productions, but in this case the criticism passed all bounds. A considerable correspondence took place in *The Times*, in which hardly anybody defended the Form. The *Church Times* said : ' As usual on such occasions, special forms of prayer have been issued by permission of ecclesiastical authority. Far beyond even what is usual, they are marked by bad literary taste and unintelligibility. They may, however, suggest some heads of intercession to priests who have the gift of translating esoteric harshness into the language of the people.' As soon as the Day of Prayer was past—on Tuesday, January 5th, a letter from Dr. Temple appeared in *The Times*, admitting that he had himself written the Form of Prayer :

' There are some (devout Christians) who desire to be assisted in the concentration of their thoughts by specific reference to the immediate occasion. The form in question was composed to meet that desire. Accordingly I quite deliberately introduced the phraseology to which exception has been taken. No doubt it could be done much better, but the introduction of " the idiom of political pamphlets " was intentional—the aim being to make it clear that the subject of political controversy is itself in this instance the subject of prayer. . . . We never use words in prayer in order to inform the Divine Mind, but always and only in order to fix our own thoughts. " Your Father knoweth what things ye have need of before ye ask Him," and so far there is no need of words at all. But with a view to realising our dependence on Him for all good things in general, and for such good things as the restoration of credit in particular, we may find it useful to employ very definite phrases, however unpoetical. William Ebor.'

A Form for Prayer for use on Sunday, January 3rd, 1932.

' Let us now pray for our country and for the world, following the pattern by which we have been taught to pray:

We draw near to Thee, Almighty God, Who hast taught us to cast all our care upon Thee:

Our Father, which art in heaven.

We are bewildered by the number and greatness of the problems before us, but our trust and hope are strong in Thee:

Our Father, which art in heaven.

Our weakness, our blindness, our selfishness hold us back from wise and courageous action ; but wisdom and power are Thine, and Thou givest them to those who truly trust in Thee:

Our Father, which art in heaven.

Through our readiness to accept cheerfully the sacrifices demanded of us for the common good :

Hallowed be Thy Name.

Through the desire of all nations and of all classes to seek fellowship one with another, and to shrink from domination, envy and distrust :

Hallowed be Thy Name.

Through the growth of unity among Christians and of goodwill among all men :

Hallowed be Thy Name. . . .

By the establishment of peace, and by the readiness of the nations to prefer justice to force :

Thy Kingdom come. . . . .

In the policy of our Government for the restoration of credit and prosperity :

Thy will be done.

In all that is done for the settlement of the future government of India :

Thy will be done.

By the restoration of commerce in the confidence of restored credit and of mutual good will :

Give us this day our daily bread.

By the co-operation of all classes in labour for the common good :

Give us this day our daily bread.

By the sympathy which gives help to the needy both at home and far away :

Give us this day our daily bread.

Because we have been selfish in our conduct of business, setting our own interest or that of our own class before the interest of others :

Forgive us our trespasses.

Because we have indulged in national arrogance, finding satisfaction in our power over others rather than in our ability to serve them.

Forgive us our trespasses.

Because we have trusted in ourselves and have neglected Thee :

Forgive us our trespasses.

If any have injured us by crooked dealing, by scamped work or by exploitation :

We forgive them that have trespassed against us.

If other countries while pursuing their own interests have unduly hindered ours :

We forgive them that have trespassed against us.

If we have suffered loss or grief through the wrongful ambition of others :

. We forgive them that have trespassed against us.

When opportunity comes to win wealth for ourselves at the cost of poverty to others :

Lead us not into temptation.

When the weakness of neighbours or rivals opens the way for us to hold them down for our advantage :

Lead us not into temptation.

When anxiety distracts the mind or prosperity lulls the conscience, and we are in danger of forgetting Thee :

Lead us not into temptation.

At times of self-satisfaction, self-seeking and self-confidence :

Deliver us from evil.

At times of boastfulness in victory, of irritation in defeat, of despair at hope deferred :

Deliver us from evil.

At times of fear concerning what others may do to us, and of desire to strike lest we ourselves be struck :

Deliver us from evil.

For over all races and nations and classes Thou rulest as King ; Thy fatherly love embraces all ; and in Thy will is our peace :

Thine is the kingdom, the power and the glory, for ever and ever. Amen.'

From a Broadcast Address on Sunday, December 27th, 1942 :

' O God our Judge and Saviour, set before us the vision of Thy purity and let us see our sins in the light of Thy countenance ; pierce our self-contentment with the shafts of Thy burning love and let love consume in us all that hinders us from perfect service of Thy cause ; for as Thy Holiness is our judgment, so are Thy wounds our salvation.'

A Blessing used by him at the end of the Mission to
Oxford University in 1931, and at many other times :

' May the love of the Lord Jesus draw you to Himself ;
   May the power of the Lord Jesus strengthen you in
      His service ;
   May the joy of the Lord Jesus fill your souls ; and
   May the blessing of God Almighty, the Father, the Son,
      and the Holy Ghost, be upon you and remain with
      you always.'

CHRIST, THE LORD OF ALL LIFE

Always, from the beginning, Temple took it for granted
that Christianity is concerned, not only with the salvation
of the individual, but with the transformation of the social
order.   Charles Gore had an abiding influence on his
thinking.   He had a large part in C.O.P.E.C., and he
was the chairman, and moving spirit, in the Malvern
Conference. Men looked to him for leadership in securing
that the ' brave new world ' should be Christian, and in
helping them to be Christians in it. He himself believed
that the nearer we come to making a Christian order,
the more essential it will be that we shall be converted
Christians, if the order is not to break down. When, as
Archbishop of Canterbury, he addressed the members of
the Bank Officers' Guild on ' The Christian View of the
Right Relationship between Finance, Production and
Consumption,' he told them :

' I was indeed most happy to receive and accept the
invitation you kindly sent me ; but not particularly because
you were a Bank Officers' Guild—I have no special
qualifications for speaking to Bank Officers—but because
I'm glad to speak to any group of people who are ready
and willing to listen concerning the place which it seems to
me their special occupation holds in the general Christian

map of life. That is my concern : to try to see the picture as it must be drawn on Christian principles, and then where the various occupations fit into it, so that those who are engaged in them, if they have the desire—which I may hope they have—to conform their practice to the Christian standard, will see where it still needs modification, where it may need even revolutionary change ; or even—very dull but sometimes salutary—where it is already perfectly sound and has only got to be kept going as it is.' Ae. p. 140.

' The Christian conception of anything is always the real essence of that thing, not some remote, Utopian and always impracticable ideal. This is primarily a theological point. If Christ were only a great moral teacher, then it might be true that what He taught was too good to be true. But if He is also the Creator of the world, then His thought of anything is what that thing truly is. Christ's conception of human nature is what human nature really is ; if we want to be severely " practical " and free from all illusions we must treat men and women after the example of Christ. So, too, industry is in fact what it is in the mind of Christ ; it is those who conduct it as if it were something else who are the illusionists.' Ab. p. 13.

' We must indeed try to reconstruct the science of Christian Sociology, and we must hope to be agreed on its main principles. But besides that we must go as individual Christians into the arena of industrial and political life, carrying those principles with us, and applying them to the actual facts and problems to the best of our ability ; and here we must not expect agreement. There is plenty of room for honest difference of opinion as regards the best way to apply Christian principles to actual conditions, and for that reason the Church should never endorse a political programme, nor become a political party, nor be attached to a political party. The Church collectively must proclaim, and also must confine itself to principles.' B. pp. 76, 77.

Because the Church must proclaim the Divine Law for

man, and the Divine Judgment, it has no option but to claim moral control in the sphere of politics and business. In our time there are four particular concerns making this urgent :

' (1) The suffering caused by existing evils makes a claim upon our sympathy which the Christian heart and conscience cannot ignore. . . . The varied forms of suffering which bad housing causes are easy to imagine in part, but few who have had no personal knowledge of it are able to imagine the whole—the crushing of a woman's pride in her home through the ceaseless and vain struggle against dirt and squalor ; the nervous fret ; the lack of home comforts for the tired worker ; the absence of any space for children to play. . . . The toleration of bad housing is a wanton and callous cruelty.

' Malnutrition is a direct result of poverty and ignorance. It produces enfeebled bodies, embittered minds and irritable spirits ; thus it tells against good citizenship and good fellowship.. Children are the most obvious sufferers, but those who have suffered in this way as children seldom come later to full strength or to physical and spiritual stability. . . .

' Unemployment is the most hideous of our social evils, and has lately seemed to have become established in a peculiarly vicious form. . . . The worst evil of such un-employment . . . is its creating in the unemployed a sense that they have fallen out of the common life. However much their physical needs may be supplied (and before the war this supply was in many cases inadequate), the gravest part of the trouble remains ; they are not wanted ! That is the thing that has power to corrupt the soul of any man not already far advanced in saintliness. Because the man has no opportunity of service, he is turned in upon himself and becomes, according to his temperament, a contented loafer or an embittered self-seeker. It has not been sufficiently appreciated that this moral isolation is the heaviest burden and most corrosive poison associated with unemployment : not bodily hunger but social futility. . . . Nothing will touch the real need except to enable the man to do something which is needed by the community. For it is part of the principle of personality that we should live for one another. . . .'

' The only real cure for unemployment is employment—beginning from the time when school education is complete and continuing, with no longer intervals than can be appreciated as holidays, till strength begins to fail. In other words we are challenged to find a social order which provides employment, steadily and generally, and our consciences should be restive till we succeed. Christian sympathy demands this.

' (2) . . . the second ground for the Church's concern in social questions (is) the educational influence of the social and economic system in which men live. This was first set forth by Plato in Books VIII and IX of the *Republic*. The social order at once expresses the sense of values active in the minds of citizens and tends to reproduce the same sense of values in each new generation. If the State is so ordered as to give great prominence to military leaders as Sparta was, as Prussia was, as Nazi Germany is, this must represent the fact that the effective body of citizens, which may be a compact minority, regards the military qualities as specially honourable or specially important ; and the system expressing that estimate impresses it by perpetual suggestion upon every growing generation. So it is if wealth receives conspicuous honour. . . .

' We throw most young Englishmen out into a world of fierce competition where each has to stand on his own feet (which is good) and fight for his own interest (which is bad), if he is not to be submerged. Our system is not deliberately planned ; but it produces effects just the same. It offers a perpetual suggestion in the direction of combative self-assertiveness. It is recognised on all hands that the economic system is an educative influence, for good or ill, of immense potency. . . . If so, then assuredly the Church must be concerned with it. For a primary concern of the Church is to develop in men a Christian character. . . . It is enough to say that the Church cannot, without betraying its own trust, omit criticism of the economic order, or fail to urge such action as may be prompted by that criticism.

' The existing system is challenged on moral grounds. . . . If the present order is taken for granted or assumed to be sacrosanct, charity from the more or less fortunate would seem virtuous and commendable ; to those for whom the order itself is suspect or worse, such charity is blood money. Why should some be in the position to dispense and others to need that kind of charity ?

' An infidel could ignore that challenge, for apart from faith in God there is really nothing to be said for the notion of human equality. Men do not seem to be equal in any respect, if we judge by available evidence. But if all are children of one Father, then all are equal heirs of a status in comparison with which the apparent differences of quality and capacity are unimportant ; in the deepest and most important of all—their relationship to God—all are equal. Why should some of God's children have full opportunity to develop their capacities in freely-chosen occupations, while others are confined to a stunted form of existence, enslaved to types of labour which represent no personal choice but the sole opportunity offered ? The Christian cannot ignore a challenge in the name of justice. . . . The moral quality of the accusation brought against the economic and social order involves the Church in " interference " on pain of betraying the trust committed to it.

' (3) For the commission given to the Church is that it carry out the purpose of God. . . . The members of the Church do not, or should not, belong to it for what they can get in this world or in any other world ; they—we—should belong to it in order to take our share in the great work, the fulfilment of God's purpose in the world and beyond it. . . .

'If we belong to the Church with such a purpose and hope as this, we are obliged to ask concerning every field of human activity what is the purpose of God for it ; If we find this purpose it will be the true and proper nature of that activity, and the relation of the various activities to one another in the divine purpose will be the " Natural Order " of those activities. To bring them into that Order, if they have, in fact, departed from it, must be one part of the task of the Church as the Body of Christ. If what has true value as a means to an end beyond itself is in fact being sought as an end in itself, the Church must rebuke this dislocation of the structure of life and if possible point out the way of recovery.   It is bound to " interfere " because it is by vocation the agent of God's purpose, outside the scope of which no human interest or activity can fall.' Ad. pp. 10–16.

THE LAW OF NATURE

'Thus, in the economic field, the reason why goods are produced is that men may satisfy their needs by consuming the goods.   Production by its own natural law exists for consumption.   If, then, a system comes into being in which production is regulated more by the profit obtainable for the producer than by the needs of the consumer, that system is defying the Natural Law or Natural Order.' Ad. p. 57.

'Evidently production does exist for the consumer, and if the consumer just won't buy it, again the process stops, and some people are prepared to accept that, and say, " Yes, but as it always is in the consumer's interest, what are you troubling about ? '' Yes, but what I want is that it should be plainly and consciously directed to the consumer's interest ; no doubt it often is, but, quite equally, no doubt, it may not be, and you may have cases where . . . there is a deliberate checking of some new process that would be immensely to the public advantage, in order to maintain the price ring for the productive concerns that are already in the field.

' But do not let us swing over at once and say that the proper thing to do is always to bring in the new thing and let the public get the benefit, because part of the public is the people engaged in those productive concerns, and when you bring the new process in you may throw them all out of work and do great damage that way. What is wanted is, of course, as usual, the whole view, the look all round, which remembers that producers themselves are in their turn consumers, and therefore, while production is for consumption, it is not true that producers exist for consumers. They are human beings, ends in themselves as much as anybody else, and the whole process must be so adjusted that in the very process of production they are able to the utmost possible extent to realise their personality and their fellowship. And so you have always got a double thing to consider at once—it is very difficult—both the wider fellowship in which the producer is related to another consumer, and the narrower one within the productive process where you want to see the same ideal human relationships reproduced so far as ever circumstances permit.' Ae. p. 153.

' It is wholesome to go back to this conception of Natural Law because it holds together two aspects of truth which it is not easy to hold in combination—the ideal and the practical. We tend to follow one or other of two lines : either we start from a purely ideal conception, and then we bleat fatuously about love ; or else we start from the world as it is with the hope of remedying an abuse here or there, and then we have no general direction or criterion of progress. The conception of Natural Law will help us to frame a conception of the right or ideal relation between the various activities of men and of the men engaged in them. For consideration of the status of an activity in the light of its social functions keeps both the ideal and the practical full in view.' Ad. p. 59.

The Archbishop's frequently expressed view that the Church—in social, political and economic concerns—must proclaim, and confine itself to, Christian principles, requires a statement of what these principles are. There are four fundamental principles, he says, which express the mind of Christ—Freedom, Membership, Service and Sacrifice :

LIBERTY

(The Sacredness of Personality.)

' First and foremost is that principle which in politics is called Liberty, but which is better represented by such a phrase as the Sacredness of Personality. This lies at the root of all our Lord's teaching about men, and all His dealing with men. It follows from the thought that God is the Father of every soul ; it is required by the fact that God is Love, and desires the love of His children. The personality of the child of God whose love God Himself desires is certainly a sacred thing. We turn to application. Does our provision of education at present correspond with a belief in the sacredness of the personality of every citizen ? (Cf. the chapter on " Education " in *Mens Creatrix*.) Or we turn to industry and economics. The text-books of Political Economy which held the field in the nineteenth century, upheld what is called the " commodity view of labour." This is the doctrine that Labour should be treated like a commodity, sold as dear as possible

H—WT

and bought as cheap as possible. But Labour is either
not a commodity at all, or else it is a unique kind of commodity ; for it is not separable from the Labourer. If I
buy a pair of boots, I do not buy the bootmaker. But if I
want to obtain a man's Labour, I must have the man ;
I must have both his body and his mind. When I hire (or
buy for a specific period) a man's labour, I hire *him*. If
then I treat Labour as a commodity, I am, so far, treating
the Labourer as a thing, not as a Person. Our industrial
system to-day does not rest on the commodity view of
Labour ; a multitude of factors have come in to modify
it. But we have not yet explicitly repudiated it or adopted
another principle in its place.' O. pp. 203, 204.

' There are two possible roots of liberty ; the one is
human selfhood, the other is divine sonship. In every
human being there is an individuality which is quite unique
and demands opportunity to express itself. So far as any
political constitution, democratic or other, rests upon a
claim to individual rights, it is rooted in this principle.
It is a principle to be treated with respect, because it represents great and explosive forces which may wreck a political
structure which makes no allowance for them. But it is not
a principle entitled to reverence, for it is merely one form
of selfishness, possibly innocent, probably noxious, and
certainly devoid of virtue. If this principle—freedom rooted
in the selfhood of the individual—obtains a complete
predominance, the result will be that form of democracy
which Plato describes in the eighth book of the *Republic*
as the worst but one of all political perversions, the worst
of all being the tyrannical state to which it gives birth as
the perversion of its own political anarchy.' AG. pp. 11, 12.

' There is, however, another form of liberty ; it is the
principle of divine sonship. The man who believes himself to be a child of God can never allow that any earthly
authority has an absolute claim to his allegiance or loyalty.
His first duty is to God, and if it seems to him that this

duty requires disobedience to earthly rulers, he will not hesitate. He must obey God rather than man. This duty will be more evident in the specifically religious sphere. The modern State was until lately tolerant in the matter of worship. But it was not always so, and it is not so everywhere to-day. Historically, the development of liberty, even in its purely political form, has been largely due to the courageous adherents of persecuted sects, who persevered in offering worship according to their consciences until the State desisted from molesting them because it found that it was dealing with forces greater than its own.' AG. p. 14. Cf. Q. p. 74.

' But though liberty of worship is the first result of the principle of divine sonship it is not the only one. For worship cannot be divorced from life without itself languishing. Special times for worship and gatherings for worship are almost futile unless they are opportunities for concentrated attention upon what gives direction to life and power to follow that direction. But if so, then liberty of worship necessarily involves for a Christian liberty to think and speak and act in such matters as those affecting the treatment of the poor, or peace and war. A liberty to pray that God's will may be done becomes a mockery if it is accompanied by a prohibition to do it. The believer in God, therefore, in claiming liberty to worship God according to his conscience is also claiming liberty to resist the State when either his conscience condemns the action of the State or the State demands of him some action which his conscience condemns.' AG. p. 15.

' If a man claims liberty, not to express himself or to promote his own interest, but to serve God, two results follow : first, he will recognise that all men are entitled to the same respect as regards their personality as himself ; and secondly, he will be more eager to resist the oppression of others than himself. . . . The love of freedom, therefore, which springs from the principle of divine sonship will appear chiefly in demands for the emancipation of others—as in the abolition of slavery—rather than in demands for the concession of fuller freedom to those who make the demands.' AG. pp. 15, 16.

' Society must be so arranged as to give to every citizen the maximum opportunity for making deliberate choices and the best possible training for the use of that opportunity. In other words, one of our first considerations will be the widest possible extension of personal responsibility ; it is the responsible exercise of deliberate choice which most fully expresses personality and best deserves the great name of freedom. Freedom is the goal of politics. To establish and secure true freedom is the primary object of all right political action. For it is in and through his freedom that a man makes fully real his personality—the quality of one made in the image of God.' Ad. p. 44.

' I am assured that this scheme (for a World Bank controlling the credit of all nations) contemplates an absolute fluidity of labour, so that people may be transferred not only from one part of their own country to another, but from their own country to another country according to the state of the market and the best opportunities of production. Now that means that you are treating human beings primarily as instruments of production ; that is simply immoral. It means that you would be ready to sacrifice richness of human personality, all the fellowships, all the traditions that grow up in the localities to which people belong ; all these loyalties that do so much to enrich life and give it its strength and its colour would be subordinated to the sheer demand of maximum economic output and maximum ease of distribution. Now efficiency of output is of very great importance, effective distribution is of very great importance, but they are important for the sake of something beyond themselves. They are important for the sake of human life, with all its qualities, and whatever restrictions may be put upon economic development by the elementary requirements of human life, have got to be accepted.' Ae. pp. 155, 156.

FELLOWSHIP

' This first principle is balanced by the second, which is the Reality of Membership. If all are children of one Father, all are members of one family. Therefore, no individual is entitled to use his liberty for his own advantage only, but should exercise it in the spirit of membership or fellowship. We may apply this also to Industry. It is sometimes urged that industry should be co-operation for public service, as if this were a remote and almost unattainable ideal. But industry never is anything else . . . the whole process goes on simply and solely because the public wants goods ; it exists for public service. And it is co-operative in its very nature. All the groups of people who take charge of the processes . . . are co-operating, whether they know it or not. And at every stage there is co-operation of the three factors—Capital, Management, and Labour. On the day that the co-operation stops, the industry stops. Industry is co-operation for public service. If, then, the people who are in it work it as if it were competition for private profit, of course it goes wrong. But our thought must be concrete, not abstract. Competition and Co-operation are logical opposites, but they are not incompatibles. . . . They may be inextricably intertwined. But it makes all the difference which is uppermost—which exercises a check upon the other. If you have the co-operative spirit uppermost, you have good sportsmen, who would rather be beaten in a good game than win in a bad one ; but if the competitive spirit is uppermost, you have men who play only to win, and will do any dirty trick that the referee will let them. So in industry our need is a full and frank recognition that industry is in its own nature fundamentally co-operative, so that all competition within it is kept in check by the co-operative spirit and purpose.' O. pp. 204, 205.

' In our Lord's teaching our relationship to God is always set forth as a family relationship ; we are children before our Father. But often we tend to think only of the relation of child and father, while ignoring the relation of child and child in the one family ; we behave as if each one were an only child. This is a form of practical polytheism, for it really involves that each has his own God.' B. p. 37.

' The Christian conception of men as members in the family of God forbids the notion that Freedom may be used for self-interest. It is justified only when it expresses itself through fellowship ; and a free society must be so organised as to make this effectual ; in other words it must be rich in sectional groupings or fellowships within the harmony of the whole.' Ad. p. 48.

' We begin, of course, with the whole conception of what, on a Christian view, human life is for : Man is created for fellowship in the family of God : fellowship first with God, and through that with all God's other children. And that is the primary test that must be applied to every system that is constructed and every change in the system that is proposed. Does it help us nearer towards fulness and richness of personal fellowship ? And fellowship, of course, is not merely the same thing as all getting together and agreeing with one another : it is compatible with a great deal of disagreement, and with a great deal of variety of experience. If you merely get together like-minded people or people with the same predominant interests in life, you don't get a fellowship ; you get a herd, which is a very inferior thing, perfectly familiar in the animal creation. It's great fun belonging to a herd—at any rate when it's hunting or doing something of that sort ; but there's nothing morally excellent about it. The herd instinct is no better in itself—or if you like, the gregarious instinct is no better in itself—than the self-regarding instinct ; it is capable of good and it is capable of bad ; and great masses of human beings have banded themselves together to do the most odious of things before now ; and the mere fact that a great number of people are united in the pursuit of an object is no sort of reason for supposing that it is a good object or that there is any merit in their union.' Ae. pp. 141, 142.

SERVICE

' The third principle which follows from these two is the Duty of Service. If I am to use my freedom in the spirit of membership in the community, it follows that I fulfil my own destiny when I make my life an act of service. Here it will suffice for illustration to refer again to the public provision for Education, and the motive which public opinion commonly supposes to be the driving force of Education and the basis of all desire for it. It cannot be denied that the notion of self-advancement—whether to spheres of service or not—plays a larger part here than Christian principle would allow. In particular, the rising generation is very inadequately trained to think of the trade or profession whereby daily bread is to be earned as the chief sphere of service ; yet if everyone exercised his trade or profession in that spirit half our problems would be solved.' O. p. 205.

' A man cannot regulate his service of his family and of his country by the Christian scale of values in its purity, first because he does not effectively accept it for himself, and secondly because his family and his country do not accept it. Nothing is so offensive as a man who applies a higher standard to other people than to himself. If a man says to his children : " I might have given you an expensive education, but decided that it would be better for you to go to the freely provided State school because my Christian principles teach me that wealth ought not to confer privilege," he must show in his whole life that he sets no store by the advantages which money can buy ; otherwise he will only be stingy and his account of his conduct will be hypocrisy, or (as we call it nowadays) " rationalisation." Now no one does accept the Christian standard for himself ; that Jesus of Nazareth did so is precisely what constitutes the gulf between Him and all other men. Only a perfect Christian can follow the purely Christian way of life ; and so far as an imperfect Christian—i.e. any Christian who actually exists—forces himself to a line of conduct which his own character does not support, it will have bad effects on both him and his neighbours : on him, because it will be an assertion of self-will and must root him more firmly than ever in his own self as centre of his life, that is in his Original Sin ; and on others because he will appear as a Pharisee and a prig, and will alienate people from the standard by which he is self-righteously guiding this part of his conduct.

' (I am finding it very hard to write this book about Christianity and the Social Order without bringing in everything else. Here I will content myself with one recollection. When a man asked St. Augustine, " What must I do to be saved ? " he answered, " Love God and do what you like "—because, of course, if he loved God he would like and could do the right thing, and if he did not love God he could not do it, however much he tried.)

' But it is not only his own defect of Christianity that a man must consider. He must not force its standard on others who are as yet unwilling or unable to receive it ; for it is of the essence of spiritual faith that it be freely accepted. If a man applies in the training of his children standards not generally accepted in their circle, and fails to bring the children themselves to accept them, the result is likely to be an alienation of the children both from their father and from his standards.

'That is one obvious illustration of the difficulty presented by the claim that Christian standards should regulate our conduct. Of course they should, but they must first regulate our souls ; and even then they are to be followed in that way—and in that way alone—which will, in fact, secure a result truly expressive of them.

'We see then why a man cannot without more ado take as his guide for the treatment of his fellows the Christian standard that service to the point of self-sacrifice is our truest welfare. Let him live by that as far as he can ; and let him invite others to join him in that enterprise ; but let him not force that standard on his fellows, and least of all on those dependent on him. They will always have the opportunity to act on it if they are so minded.' Ad. pp. 52, 53.

THE POWER OF SACRIFICE

'This leads us on to the fourth principle, which is the most distinctive of the Christian scheme—the Power of Sacrifice. What is the driving power of progress ? The natural man thinks it can be accomplished by force. But force alone achieves nothing positive, because it does not convert heart or will. Force has its place. It is right to use force in order to prevent other force doing positive harm. Such is the use of force represented by the police. But this function of force is purely negative. It prevents harm from being done, and so leaves the way open for real progress. This comes not by force but by sacrifice. . . . I should be ready to affirm that so far as real progress has been won by means of strikes, it has never been really due to the inconvenience caused to employers or to the public, but to the sympathy called out by the endurance of the strikers, and (still more) to a realisation of the justice of their cause to which their endurance may call attention. We may apply this principle, and the last, to international

questions. How far do we think of our national greatness
as consisting in the power to dictate to other countries,
and how far as consisting in service rendered to mankind
even at loss to ourselves ? ' O. p. 206.

DEMOCRACY

' There has been a great deal of fustian talked about
democracy : *vox populi vox Dei* : what nonsense ! The
defence of government by a majority is not that the majority
is always right ; on the contrary, the only thing you know
for certain about a majority with regard to any new issue
is that it's sure to be a little wrong. Only you have no
earthly means of finding out which of the minorities, if
any, is right ; and it is very unlikely that the majority will
be as wrong as some of the minorities are likely to be.
Therefore, it is a great deal safer to let the majority rule
than the minority. That's a dull pedestrian argument,
isn't it ? But, of course, the real defence of democracy
is not that at all—it is not in that region. It is that by calling
upon people to exercise responsible judgment on the matters
before the country at any time, you develop their personal
qualities. You make them feel that they belong to one
another in this corporate society, and so you tend to
deepen and intensify personal fellowship. You are leading
people forward from the relationship of the herd to that
of real fellowship by the mere process of calling upon them
to take their share in the government of the groups of
which they are members. That is the real value of the thing,
its educational effect upon the citizens, and through that,
of course, you get a more alert, a more disciplined intelligence in the citizens—less liable to be swayed by mass
hysteria and the like—less likely to be victims of pro-
paganda, one of the subtle perils of democracy at all times—
and through that once more you will get, in the long run,

a wider and a better government because it is government by wiser and better citizens. But it must always be through that line of argument, it seems to me—at least on Christian grounds—that we defend democracy. It is because it gives the highest value, higher than any other political scheme, to the personality and the personal relationships of all the citizens in the community.' AE. pp. 142, 143.

' It has been historically the sense of the dignity of every individual which has mainly contributed to the impulse towards democracy, political and social. Democracy so regarded is a definitely Christian product. . . . You do not find it anywhere in the world except where Christianity has exerted its influence. But not only is it a Christian product as a matter of fact, but it is a necessary result of Christianity in the long run as a matter of principle, because it is Christianity that discovered the real meaning of personality ; or, to speak more correctly, it was in and through Christianity that the real meaning of personality was revealed. There is no word for personality in Greek or Latin. . . . It was through the revelation of what the life of the Spirit is in the activity of God towards men, in the relationship of men to God, and, under that, of men to one another, that the conception of personality grew up.' Q. pp. 76–78.

' The Equality that is precious is not equality of powers or gifts, which does not exist, nor an equality of influence or authority ; it is an equality of inherent worth and of the right of every individual to be himself. . . . It is perfectly compatible with Equality rightly understood that some should command and some should obey, and all that we need to purge such a view of all that may make it embitter-ing is to recognise that to obey is quite as noble as to command. The one true form of Equality politically is equality of opportunity.' Q. pp. 81, 82.

' There is, in fact, only one safe course for democracy, and that is that it should recognise its source in Christianity and allow Christian principles at all points to govern it. This will, of course, involve a great tenderness towards anything that can fairly be represented as a point of conscience . . . for it is the recognition that the real meaning of society is to be found in the true spiritual freedom of the citizens. If we keep steadily in mind the fact that citizens are children of God, who owe an allegiance certainly to their country, but who can never make that allegiance either absolute or primary because there is a higher authority, namely God Himself, to Whom, in the last resort, and to Whom alone, their complete submission is due, then democracy will find the proper check which will save it from ever becoming such a mere tyranny of majorities as it was in the worst days of the French Revolution. Democracy, in fact, must be regarded as merely the outward form, within which the spirit of the Christian religion may most effectively work in the hearts of men.' Q. pp. 85, 86.

" Rights and duties, broadly speaking, are correlative terms ; it is your duty to respect my rights, it is my duty to respect your rights. It might, therefore, be supposed that for all to be concerned with their rights and for all to be concerned with their duties would have much the same result. But in fact we seldom agree on the question what our rights actually are, and the mental habit of insisting on them always leads to an exaggeration of them. When we are really concerned with duties, a wholly different atmosphere is created, and democracy will become a means, not of bitter competition and rivalry of sections, but of wider fellowship and a truer brotherhood than can be achieved by any other means.' Q. pp. 98, 99.

' Perhaps there is nothing so important for our modern democracy as to learn this transference of emphasis from rights to duties.' As. p. 65.

' Every degraded wretch of whom society despairs is a soul that God created as an object of His love, and died (or eternally dies) to win to loving fellowship with Himself. A social doctrine or system which aims at being in accordance with facts will deal with every human being as of unique and irreplaceable value, because he is a child of God. And this involves two consequences. First, there must be the best possible chance for the development of all gifts and faculties ; or, in other words, every child is entitled to the best procurable education. Secondly, there must be the widest possible area of effective choice, for it is in actual choice that personality manifests its most distinctive features.' Ab. p. 9.

' Here is the real root of Democracy. We must find some way of recognising that each individual citizen is no tool to be made use of for the attainment of some prosperity in which he will not share, still less mere cannon fodder, but is a living personality, with mind and heart and will, who can only be himself so far as he freely thinks and feels and plans. The root of Democracy is respect for individual personality.

' At this point Democracy closely touches Christianity, which teaches the infinite worth of every individual. Democracy is just one, almost certainly the fullest and best, way of showing respect for the individual in the political constitution ; majority rule is the one device for giving constitutional weight to the judgment of the ordinary man. Its justification is not that the majority is sure to be right, for it is much more likely to be partly wrong ; not that it is efficient, for up to date that has not been conspicuously true ; but that it does honour to the ordinary citizen and helps to develop his personality. In short, its justification is to be its educational efficiency.' Ab. pp. 73, 74.

' By three tests it can be known whether Democracy is true to its own root principle : by the depth of its concern for justice to individuals ; by the careful regard which it pays to the rights of minorities ; by the scrupulous respect which it offers to whatever can present itself in the name of individual conscience. Of these the last is the most vital of all. Society may have to protect itself against fanatical faddists ; but respect to the conscientious objector is, broadly speaking, a hall-mark of true democracy.' Ab. p. 77.

' But the Church will also perpetually insist that personality in man is derivative, not original, and only deserves the recognition claimed for it so far as it recognises itself as dependent on the Personality of God. Consequently its exercise must correspond with the known character of God. The revelation through which we know God as fully personal, also sets Him before us as righteous, self-sacrificing love. Now what has mainly spoilt democratic movements in the past has been that they have rested on the assertion of rights rather than duties, and even when the rights asserted are true and just, the assertion of them creates an ungodly, because unlovely, frame of mind. The whole notion of rights belongs to the world of claims and counter-claims, the world below the level of fellowship. But the notion of duties at once lifts us to that level, and increasingly so as the divine spirit of love becomes the mainspring of our performance of duty.

' Democracy is akin to Christianity ; but Christianity is a great deal more than Democracy. It lifts it to its true origin, which is faith not primarily in Man but primarily in God, and in Man because he was made to be a child of God, and member of God's family. Nothing in Democracy itself requires to be changed in the process of its spiritualisation, but very much in most democrats must be changed. And only in the degree in which that change takes place, only in the degree in which democrats put duty before rights and recognise that the rights of human personality are derived from its dependence on and relation to the divine Personality, can Democracy become the ideal form of society or be secured against the danger of degenerating into the worst.' Ab. p. 80.

" The appointed task of modern civilisation is to devise some method of organising the community in such a way as to dispense with the institution of slavery. This task has not yet been accomplished except nominally ; and its nominal accomplishment amounts to no more in fact than the recognition that its accomplisheent is desirable. The achievement of that consummation would seem to be itself the establishment of the kingdom of heaven or, at any rate, of its economic machinery, for it will be the establishment of a society whose charter is that all its citizens share alike its blessings ; and beyond universality it is clearly impossible to go. The task of modern civilisation is then the last and hardest task that confronts man as a political being. Whether or not it is possible for a single nation to realise this ideal for itself I do not propose to discuss ; it may be that war, either actual or possible, is a fatal obstacle, and that the problem of organising the state is dependent on that of organising the world.' AH. p. 1.

' For the science of politics, at any rate, the essence of slavery is this, that men are regarded as a means of production, and not as ends in themselves ; that their economic value as productive agents is considered, and that their welfare as spiritual beings is not.' AH. p. 2.

' The social problem is perennial. And the social problem does not consist of slums, or of excessive numbers of public houses ; these are symptoms and aggravations of the problem, but the problem itself lies deeper. Perhaps at the present moment it may be summed up thus : education is no longer the privilege of a single class ; the poorer classes have obtained an education ; they have begun to think ; and the constitution—social and industrial as well as political—is slowly and with much effort adapting itself to this new and most perplexing fact. The social problem is, therefore, the conflict of the ideas held by the various classes about each other and about society, and of the means by which they attempt to realise those ideas. Now, our constitution and the conservative instincts of human nature retain power for the most part in the hands of the wealthier classes ; and, if they are enlightened, the transition, which the progress of the poorer classes has rendered inevitable, will be effected smoothly and without disaster. But what has happened ?   The ruling class, indolent, ignorant and secure, suddenly awoke at about the time of the first Jubilee to find that working men had banded themselves together to conspire against their masters, and tyrannically prevented honest souls from gaining a miserable pittance by continuing to work when a strike had been ordered. That was how many respectable citizens regarded Trade Unions at the time of the early strikes—most of all, perhaps, at the time of the London Dock Strike—and that was how they regarded the inevitable policy of picketing, which it seems is to be legalised at last. Of course the Unions have abused their power ;   of course there have been deplorable excesses. But surely that is the fault of the ruling classes who could not read the signs of the times, who never gave the industrial revolution a thought until it began to assert itself with vigour and to " ruffle the ocean of their self-control". But still it is not too late ; still it is possible for us to learn to understand how the working class regard us, and what kind of society they wish to substitute for the existing one.   When we understand it, perhaps it will attract us too, and then we can help them to realise it, or perhaps we shall think it can be improved, and then we can make intelligent efforts to modify their schemes. But we can do nothing while we are ignorant of the new ideas and the new methods, ignorant even of those great industrial organisations of which Professor Ashley not unreasonably speaks as " among the greatest contributions of this country to the progress of civilisation". And while we do nothing we shall incur the enmity of those whose progress is checked by our inactivity, and so the social body will be divided against itself.

'And worse than this : inasmuch as knowledge and culture are, to some, a monopoly of the wealthier classes, these, the highest fruits of civilisation, will also be regarded by the party of progress as hostile to their aims ; the rising power in the state will reject those virtues whose production is the state's chief function ; and the blame will lie at our doors.' AH. pp. 15–17.

SEX

' To use that function of our nature as an opportunity of passing amusement always involves treating another person as a plaything or a toy. That is destructive of the freedom we are fighting to maintain, for the heart of that freedom is the dignity of personality. But here . . . the religious background makes all the difference in the world. There is nothing nasty about sex as God has made it ; there is no reason why it should not be spoken of in a natural and matter-of-fact way ; but it must be treated with respect and even with reverence, because it is the means by which men and women are enabled to act on behalf of God in the creation of His children, which is why parents are said to procreate. The reason for not joking about sex is exactly the same as for not joking about the Holy Communion. It is not that the subject is nasty, but that it is sacred, and to joke about it is profanity. Moreover, it is the point at which the spiritual and the physical come into closest interplay, and this no doubt is why moralists normally take it as the example of the moral struggle. Sexual sin is not the only sin nor the worst kind of sin ; the supreme sin and the fountain-head of all the others is pride, not lust. But if we let this function be used for our pleasure and amusement we are spoiling one of the most splendid things in the world.' Ae. p. 75.

' This is an age of revolt. Popular sympathy is with the

rebel, not with the upholder of law. The argument for allowing persons separated from their wives to marry others is chiefly that they very much desire to do so. And our generation tends to think that if anyone wants very much to do a thing, he ought to be allowed. The upholder of law against passion is regarded as stuffy, conventional, tyrannical. This is wholesome as a reaction from a conventionalism that ignores human values ; but it is disastrous as a basis for public policy. When once the question is asked, it is clear that the fostering of happy marriages is socially far more important than the remedying of unhappy ones. That does not mean that the latter can be ignored ; but, while it claims consideration, it comes second and not first.' Ab. p. 117.

Probably no evil infesting our national life is more disastrous than venereal disease, and the problem of how to tackle it is supremely difficult. It is safe to say that nearly all clerical references to the subject are fatuously abstract and unreal. In 1943 the Archbishop delivered an address on the Church's approach to this problem to a conference convened by the Central Council for Health Education. It is masterly, and should be read by everyone. Some extracts follow :

' Where spiritual, moral, social, and medical aspects are all discoverable in one fact or tendency, they should receive attention in that order ; or, to put it concretely, inasmuch as the problem before us is both moral and physical, the moral element in it is the more important and should have the first attention.' Ae. p. 66.

' The first question we have to ask about any proposed action in this field is, " What suggestion is it offering ? "— not—" What result does it aim at ? " or, " What inducements or penalties does it provide ? " but, " What suggestion will it make ? "

' It is a fundamental principle of far-reaching importance that Governments affect the conduct of their subjects far more by the principles implicit in their acts than by the requirements of legislation or of the severity of the penalties attached to neglect of those requirements. Thus the earlier attempts to put down crimes of violence and various kinds of theft by means of savage punishment were a total failure. The callousness in inflicting pain, or the readiness to take life displayed by the Government, encouraged these bad qualities in its subjects more than the penalties restrained them. To bring this home to the legislators of his generation was one of the great achievements of Jeremy Bentham.

' In dealing with venereal disease our rulers systematically ignore this principle. Thus in the Army, with a view to checking venereal disease, instruction is given to recruits in the use of prophylactics. The implication and suggestion is that the authorities expect a considerable number to practise fornication. There is no doubt at all in my own mind—though proof is evidently impossible—that this method, by its inevitable suggestion, causes an increase of promiscuous intercourse, and, therefore, also an increase of the disease which it is designed to prevent. And the root trouble is the treatment of what is primarily a moral problem as if it were primarily a medical problem.' Ae. pp. 67, 68.

EDUCATION

William Temple inherited from his father a passionate interest in education and, in particular, in that kind of educational reform which consists in securing more and better education for those who in these respects have been neglected in the past :

' Every child should have the opportunity of an education till years of maturity, so planned as to allow for his peculiar aptitudes and make possible their full development. This education should throughout be inspired by faith in God and find its focus in worship.' Ad. p. 73.

' We are not training children according to their own true nature or in relation to their true environment unless we are training them to trust in God. In their own nature they are God's children, destined for eternal fellowship with Him, and their environment exists at three levels—the sub-human, studied in the Natural Sciences ; the human, studied in the Humanities ; and the super-human, studied in Divinity. The school must provide for all three.' Ad. p. 69.

' The development of individual gifts under a predominant motive of self-seeking is an injury both to the individual and to the society. Plato saw this perfectly clearly. It was only those who had been moulded by his moral training who would in his ideal Republic be allowed to receive higher intellectual equipment. In other words, if a man is going to be a knave, it is desirable both for society and for himself that he should also be a fool. To quicken the wits of those who will afterwards use them to prey upon their neighbours is an evident injury to society, but it is a still greater injury to them.' Ad. p. 67.

' The main ground for raising the school age is often obscured by other considerations which are important in their place, but are essentially secondary. This main ground is the necessity of providing a social life or community in which the individual may feel that he has a real share and for which he may feel some genuine responsibility. If a child is thrown out into the world at fourteen or even fifteen with nothing to which he may belong between him and the national community, or even his city or county, that is too large a body for him to realize in it anything like living membership. He needs a society of people about his own age, in the activities of which he may take a share equal to that of any other member, so that it may reasonably claim his loyalty, and he may have the sense of being wanted in it. Nothing else will draw out from him the latent possibilities of his nature. . . . Of course it is true that if the school leaving age is to be raised, we need a far more varied type of education, and for a great many, probably the large majority, this ought to consist much more in various forms of manual activity than in the extraction of information from printed books ; there might be a system of apprenticeship to various industries, including agriculture, under the supervision of the Local Education Authority and its officers. But there is no chance of our developing this varied curriculum, or training teachers to handle it, until the thing begins to be done. We must start with inadequate equipment and then make it more adequate as we go on. When once it is granted that the main need of a young citizen is a living fellowship of other young citizens within which the greater part of his time shall be spent, criticisms of the available forms of curriculum become irrelevant to the main issue. If we are going to show a real respect to each individual as a child of God, we must see that from infancy to full maturity every child is set in such a social context as will best develop all the powers which God has given him. To provide such an opportunity, not for a favoured few but for all children, is an urgent national duty. To fail here on the ground of the large expenditure required would be a national sin.' Ad. pp. 65, 66.

TOLERATION

William Temple had a unique conviction of the essential importance of toleration, and he practised it unfalteringly. I remember him saying that it would be useless for men to pool their thoughts unless they differed ; and he wrote an Introduction to a pamphlet by Mr. Stephen Hobhouse *because* he disagreed with what he said in it.

' The whole forward movement of our social life turns on the development among the great mass of the people of that kind of education which makes men eager both to think for themselves and to appreciate the truth in any opinion from which they dissent.' Ab. p. 76.

' Can we find a phrase to sum up what is required of us in the circumstances of our time ? May we not say that our obligation is to lay aside all other partisanship and become partisans of good-will ? Of course we shall still have our own convictions about what is true and our own judgments about what is expedient ; and these differences will lead us to associate with different groups or parties in Church or State. But we shall choose our party, never for the retaining or gaining or advantage for ourselves, but solely according to our understanding of the general good ; in all controversy our aim will be to appreciate and incorporate in our own theory or action all that we can find good or wise in the views of our opponents. We shall strive for the truth as we have seen it, but shall never suppose that there is no truth but what we have seen, and we shall believe that fellowship and goodwill are worth more than any triumph of our own opinions, because only in such fellowship can be found the fuller truth than that which the various disputants possess. The only thing not immoral which we shall refuse to tolerate is intolerance, and even with that we shall try to sympathise, while we condemn it.

' The goodwill of which we should be partisans, amid all the conflict of self-assertive and self-seeking parties, is no placid amiability ; it is the love which truly counts the sorrows of others as our own. If we loved our neighbours as ourselves, we should think it as dreadful that our neighbour's children should be brought up in slums as that ours should be. The misery of many of our coal fields, the continued depression due to bad trade, the inequalities of educational opportunity, and the whole treatment by our country of a great part of its adolescent population would torment our consciences." Au. An Address to the Laity.

' One great gain that the scientific use of the comparative method in religion has brought us is the duty of genuine reverence for other men's beliefs. To reverence them is not at all the same thing as to accept them as necessarily true, but whatever thoughts any human soul is seeking to live by, deserve the reverence of every other human soul ; and the comparative method of religion is the intellectual expression of that belief." P. p. 22.

CONCLUSION

' Force has its place in resisting evil which force threatens to inflict; it was right (as I think) to resist by force the forcible aggression of Germany. It may be right for Labour to resist by force a forcible aggression of Capital. But real progress comes by self-sacrifice. In a society that had never become corrupted, fellowship might rest on justice ; but when once corruption has set in, it can only be based on self-sacrifice. The voluntary suffering of the innocent is the healing balm for the wounds of the world. When nations are ready to suffer rather than risk the sin of aggression, when Labour and Capital are ready to suffer rather than risk receiving unrighteous gain, when all of us are ready to suffer rather than risk the wickedness of consuming more than we contribute—then, and not till then, will men have rest from their troubles. The Cross is the means of salvation.

' " But this puts off for ever all hope of a solution ; you are impracticable ; you are a dreamer."

' If so, then Christ was a deluded fanatic and His religion is a fraud.

' " But what you propose is impossible ; you cannot alter human nature."

' No ; but God can ; and Christ was born and died and rose again and sent the Holy Spirit to do that very thing.' Ab. p. 18.

NOTE

The publishers and/or editors of the following books are thanked for permission to quote from them. They are referred to in this book by the letters attached to them in this list.

A. *Basic Convictions.* Hamish Hamilton, 1937.

B. *Personal Religion and the Life of Fellowship.* The Bishop of London's Lent Book for 1926. Longmans.

C. *Repton School Sermons.* Macmillan, 1913.

D. *War Primer* containing Prayers for use in time of war: edited by Canon F. B. Macnutt. S.P.C.K.

E. *York Quarterly.*

F. *York Diocesan Leaflet.*

G. *Canterbury Diocesan Gazette and Notes.*

H. *Readings in St. John's Gospel.* 2 Vols. Macmillan, 1939, 1940.

J. *Fellowship with God.* Sermons at Westminster Abbey and elsewhere. Macmillan, 1920.

K. *Studies in the Spirit and Truth of Christianity.* University and School Sermons. Macmillan, 1914.

L. *Mens Creatrix.* An Essay. Macmillan, 1923.

M. *Nature, Man and God.* The Gifford Lectures in Glasgow, 1932–1934. Macmillan.

N. *The Province of Science.* An Essay. Printed for Private Circulation, 1904.

O. *Christus Veritas.* An Essay. Macmillan, 1924.

P. *The Universality of Christ.* Student Christian Movement, 1921.

Q. *Christ in His Church.* The Primary Visitation Charge in the Diocese of Manchester. Macmillan, 1924.

R. *Creation and Redemption.* The University Sermon at Cambridge, Septuagesima, 1925. Cambridge Review.

S.   *Scientific Ideas among the Ancient Greeks.* A Paper read to the Repton School Scientific Society by the Headmaster, 1911.

T.   *Poetry and Science.*   In Essays and Studies by Members of the English Association, Vol. xvii, Second Series. Oxford, 1932.

U.   *Social Witness and Evangelism.* The Beckly Lecture. The Epworth Press, 1943.

V.   *The Resources and Influence of English Literature.* The National Book Council, 1942.

W.   *Robert Browning.* An Essay (W. T.). Printed for Private Circulation, 1904.

Y.   *Christianity and the State.* Scott Holland Memorial Lecture. Macmillan, 1928.

Z.   *More Points of View.* Allen and Unwin, 1930.

Aa. *The Kingdom of God.* Macmillan, 1912.

Ab. *Essays in Christian Politics and Citizenship and Kindred Subjects.* Longmans, 1927.

Ac. *The Manchester Diocesan Magazine.*

Ad. *Christianity and Social Order.* Penguin Special, 1942.

Ae. *The Church Looks Forward.* Macmillan, 1944.

Af. *The Nature of Personality.* Macmillan, 1911.

Ag. *The Idea of God.* An Article in *The Spectator,* April, 1931.

Ah. *Back to Unity. The University of Toronto Quarterly,* October, 1934.

Ai. *Thoughts on Problems of the Day.* The Primary Visitation Charge in the Diocese of York. Macmillan, 1931.

Aj. *Christianity as an Interpretation of History.* William Ainslie Memorial Lecture. Longmans, 1945.

Ak. *Blackfriars.* A monthly review edited by the English Dominicans.

Ao. *The York Journal of Convocation.*

Aq. *The Christian Hope of Eternal Life.* S.P.C.K.

Ar. *Foundations.* A statement of Christian Belief in Terms of Modern Thought. By Seven Oxford Men. Macmillan, 1912.

As. *Plato and Christianity.* Macmillan, 1916.

Au. *Enthronement Addresses at York.* 1929.

Av. *Christian News-Letter.*

Aw. *Unto This Last.* A Sermon preached in Repton School Chapel, 1915.

Ax. *Palm Sunday to Easter.* S.C.M., 1942.

Ay. *Abstract Speculation.* First Paper for the Jowett Society, 1901.

Az. Introduction to *The Teaching Church,* edited by A. L. Woodward. S.P.C.K., 1928.

AA. *The Fellowship of the Holy Spirit.* A National Mission Pamphlet, S.P.C.K., 1917.

AB. *A Living Church.* Life and Liberty Papers, No. ii, S.P.C.K.

AC. *The Genius of the Church of England.*

AD. *The Church and Its Teaching To-Day.* Noble Lectures at Harvard. Macmillan, 1936.

AE. *The Review.* The Magazine of the G.D.A., September, 1932.

AF. *The Ethics of Punishment.* The John Howard Anniversary Sermon. The Howard League for Penal Reform, 1945.

AG. *Faith and Freedom.* Broadcast National Lecture, 1935.

AH. *The Education of Citizens.* An Address to the Parents' National Educational Union, 1905.

AN INTRODUCTION TO
THE BIBLE

STANLEY COOK

(Pelican Book A 144)

A general introduction to the Bible and Apocrypha in the light of modern research. It describes how we got the English Bible, and the prior stages from the earliest known original sources. It briefly surveys the contents of the Bible, and deals more fully with the leading ideas that make the book a whole.

A chapter on Jerusalem and Mount Zion indicates how the ancient and mysterious city came to hold its place in Judaism and Christianity.

Some fundamental biblical problems are outlined, and there are two chapters on understanding and teaching the Bible.

There is a chapter on other "Bibles" and sacred lore, and an Epilogue on the bearing of the Bible on the present situation.

Chronological and bibliographical notes and an index are provided.

"For concentrated information about the Bible, it would be impossible to surpass Prof. Cook's new Pelican book." —*Theology*.

"Behind the book lie a wealth of learning, a richness of spiritual understanding and a knowledge of the world. The book reads well and is more entertaining than many a work of fiction."—*Western Mail*.

"Just the volume about the Bible which one could put into the hands of the ordinary layman with confidence."— *Christian World*.

THE REBIRTH OF CHRISTIANITY

STANLEY COOK

A 116

THIS BOOK, on the world-crisis in the history of religious and other thought, is written in the conviction that Christianity alone can inaugurate a new and better order, but that it must be re-stated if it is to have any cultural influence. This conviction involves a reconsideration of the place of the Bible in universal history and religion, and of the light thrown by the comparative and historical study of religions upon the development of ideas of what is most real and true.

It involves also the current reconsideration of nature and man and of the processes that operate in both, ranging from those in physics and biology to those more essential processes of the mind that enable man to understand something of his universe and to face the future. Critical, but with a firm hold upon the values of religion, it stresses the realism of an effective religion, and believes that the best "theory" of the cosmic processes in general is that which best understands its rivals and opponents.

The book takes a fresh and independent line which will probably please neither those who are satisfied with their own religion or with the present religious situation, nor those who practically assign an absolute priority to scientific, economic and social problems, and regard man as the sole master of his evolution.

"For all who look and work for religious renascence to-day this is a book to study and possess."—Theology.

"It is difficult to decide what is most deserving of praise in this book—the originality of its viewpoint, the depth of its scholarship, or the fearlessness with which it faces the great problems of life . . . definitely a book deserving study, and also the grateful thanks of every lover of Christianity."—Religions.

LOCAL GOVERNMENT
IN ENGLAND & WALES

W. E. JACKSON

This book will interest everyone who wants to have, without elaborate technicalities, a plain statement of what local government is all about. It provides, by an author of unusually varied experience, a simplified but authentic explanation of what the local government system is, its place in the national scheme, and what the various types of local council do and the numerous and important public services they perform. The citizen who wishes to keep informed on public affairs, or the student who is looking for something easier than the duller text books, will find this book of value. Even the member or official of a local authority will find it useful as a compendious refresher course and a companion for brief and easy reference. There is a short historical sketch showing how modern administration has developed out of the ancient forms, certain features of which still survive and lend colour to local affairs. There is a masterly résumé of the wide range of services carried on by local authorities, with summaries in tabular form showing the main functions of each class of authority. The special position of London is dealt with.

The administration of justice in boroughs and counties is shortly described. An account is given of the procedure at local elections, with the qualifications and disqualifications for voting and for being elected. The reader is given an insight into local government from within, the organisation of departments and committees, the general method of carrying on business, its comparison with parliamentary and normal commercial practice, and the procedure at council and committee meetings. The effect of politics in local government is alluded to.

There is a chapter about municipal officials and the work they do, the prospects of local government as a career, and the salaries and conditions of service. The relative positions of the elected member and the official are discussed. The author pays special tribute to the voluntary work done by the elected member. Another chapter is devoted to local government finance, the rating system, government grants, local loans and trading services, showing where the local authority gets its money, and the procedure in spending it.

The legal responsibilities of local authorities towards each other, towards the individual citizen and to the central government are briefly surveyed and the future trends and the possible effect of the great reforms now pending are outlined.

A Pelican Book (A 162)

JUVENILE DELINQUENCY AND THE LAW

A. E. JONES

(Pelican Book A 158)

"This is a thoughtful and interesting book. It throws much new light on one of the biggest problems of the day."—*John Bull*.

"The book is well worth anybody's shilling for the hundred pages alone, which tell us what the young delinquent is, where he comes from, who deals with him and what methods of dealing with him are available."—*Friend*.

"Unwearyingly bright in its style, but underlying its facetious phrases is real understanding interest in the tragedy implicit in every case of serious delinquency."—*New Statesman*.

"He is informative and he has a point of view. First he discusses the factors, sociological and psychological, which play a part in determining delinquency. After dealing with the causes of delinquency, he proceeds to give an account of the background of the legislation of 1908 and 1933, taking the line that it should be regarded as a reaction against the inhumanities of past generations; then he goes on to describe the Juvenile Court and its ambiguous functions, providing a refuge for those sinned against, and determining treatment for the sinner; finally he considers the treatments at the disposal of the Court."—*Listener*.

"Mr. Jones' personal views are stated with studied moderation. . . . His book is thoughtful and provocative and is a really useful contribution to the discussion of an important and difficult subject."—*New English Weekly*.

Pelican Book.